Wear

THE

Crown

*Living in Your Royal Identity
as a Daughter of the King*

MELODY JOY DAVIS

Wear the Crown

Trilogy Christian Publishers
A Wholly Owned Subsidiary of Trinity Broadcasting Network
2442 Michelle Drive, Tustin, CA 92780

10 9 8 7 6 5 4 3 2 1

Library of Congress Cataloging-in-Publication Data is available.

ISBN 979-8-89041-274-4
ISBN 979-8-89041-275-1 (ebook)

DEDICATION

This book is dedicated to my parents.

Thank you, Mom,
for providing an atmosphere of unconditional love,
care, and safety in which to grow up.
Without that, I don't believe I could have
written this particular book.

Having been loved well by an earthly father
is a gift, for it most certainly shapes
our understanding of our heavenly Father.
Dad, you have been *my* gift for fifty-five years.

ACKNOWLEDGMENTS

Thank you to my husband for twenty-eight years of lavishing love on me.

I'm convinced you have always seen the invisible crown I wear because you have always treated me like a queen.

Thank you to Val for seeing my capabilities more clearly than I could at times. Through the Heritage Singers platform, your leadership encouraged me to develop other gifts God wanted me to use. Your enthusiastic encouragement and belief in me gave me the courage to grow.

TABLE OF CONTENTS

PROLOGUE:
She

"Breathe… just breathe…"

Something she had to remind herself of more and more these days. Mind jumbled, heart racing, body aching — over time, these sensations had become the new normal without her even realizing it.

But today she felt it. She felt it all.

The critics were loud. The ones who said, without words, how ugly and inadequate she was, how she would never be one of "them." Critics everywhere. The ones inside her head, the worst of them all.

The powerful ones with their upper hand required warrior-like stealth and vigilance that left her in perpetual exhaustion. Always on the lookout for the advantage-takers and the dismissers.

The responsibilities seemed to always outweigh the capabilities. The to-do list was always one step forward, two steps back. The ones who needed her most often got the worst of her because there was never enough, and the guilt of lack weighed heavy.

Lack of patience, kindness, and joy. Anxiety outweighed peace; frustration outweighed contentment. "When will I ever be enough?"

INTRODUCTION

Never enough. Our world has been seared with the hot iron of "never enough." Never enough time. Never enough money. Never enough hands to juggle all the plates that are too full anyway.

If you're like most women in today's American culture, you may find yourself way too acquainted with stress and anxiety from the mounting pressures of life. Those two thieves are like friends you never wanted who somehow appeared out of nowhere and grabbed hold of you with a relentless grip. You just can't get rid of them, so instead you get used to them. And after a while they become so familiar, they don't even register as annoying anymore, just normal.

Stress, anxiety, fear, and worry affect everyone. It doesn't matter who you are; the pressures of life are everywhere, and they feel inescapable most of the time. The pressures of marriage and family, career, and finances. The pressures of being single or single parenting. The pressure to find the perfect spouse or to stick it out with the one you already have. The pressure of all the responsibilities we find ourselves carrying. The expectations we try to live up to — our own and everyone else's. The pressure to be physically attractive. To achieve and be successful. To fit in and stay relevant. The pressure from regretting the past and fearing the future.

We don't want to live this way, but we often think there's no other way to live. It's just how it is and how it goes. Life is hard, but what choice do we really have? Then there is the added pressure of our "life of faith." We've been born again, attend church, have a "quiet time" — when we can squeeze it in — and maybe even attend a small group or Bible study. Yet, something inside us senses that something is missing. We were meant for more. But we settle for less.

How do we do this thing called the Christian life when life can be so hard? We've heard that Jesus said, "I came that they may have life and have it abundantly" (John 10:10, ASV). But what does that really mean? We've heard all the spiritual talk about living a "victorious life in Christ." But how do we do that for real? We ignore the questions because we don't know the answers.

A lot of believers feel stuck on autopilot. They feel disillusioned or discouraged. And let's face it, being a Jesus follower in a world that is becoming increasingly hostile to the things of God is intimidating.

Many of you are tired. You have been running on empty for too long, and it has taken its toll. Women today are bombarded with unrealistic expectations and harsh admonishments. Criticism and conflicting messages are rampant. Standards of beauty are nearly impossible to attain. The current call to arms is "empowerment" — that we *can* and *should* be "empowered women"! And not only that, but we also can and should be "women who empower women"!

These declarations of strength, individuality, passion, and power sound fantastic and liberating, but sometimes they're just plain confusing, seemingly unattainable, and ironically, another source of pressure.

By this point you may be asking, "Okay, so what's your point? Better yet, what's the solution?" The short answer is this…

It's time to really discover the kingdom of God.

CHAPTER 1:
Wear the Crown

I am a princess not because I have a prince, but because my Father is a King.

— Kim Laminen

When I was little, I loved to play dress up, and when I did, I always wanted to wear the pretty things, the glamorous things. I could make anything beautiful: an old nightgown or an old hat, at least in my imagination. I would always pretend to be the queen or the princess or the beautiful heroine. I don't think I ever dressed up in ugly rags pretending to be a beggar on the side of the road — like the ones I imagined from Bible stories — not because they weren't loved; Jesus was crazy about those people… it's because I really didn't like their outfits.

To imagine a king or a queen, to imagine a kingdom, conjures up visions of fairytales and make-believe. Our modern Western culture has no practical context for kings and kingdoms. But in Jesus' day, they did.

I'm sure that when many of you hear "kingdom of God," your minds go straight to the "land of make-believe." But the kingdom of God is not make-believe. It's not an esoteric idea or a poetic metaphor. It's a very real realm of absolute perfection and power, beauty, and love, where no one is a beggar.

It is a kingdom realm over which God is the King, and every believer a citizen. Please note I didn't say "will be" a citizen, as in "after we die," but rather *is* a citizen even now. I don't think that concept is natural for our brains to easily accept or comprehend, but the ramifications of truly believing it and understanding all that means are huge. We may not yet live in the *fullness* of the kingdom of God. That's obvious. But, as followers of Jesus, we *have become* citizens of that kingdom nonetheless.

God is constantly and faithfully interacting with His redeemed and intervening on our behalf. When the Holy Spirit is moving and working in our lives and in the world around us, *this* is the kingdom realm breaking through the darkness into the earth realm bit by bit. The Spirit of God in us is how we can recognize the "unseen" kingdom of heaven and give thanks for it.

We're all familiar with the concept of heaven, our eternal dwelling place and the final destination of those who have received the gift of salvation and been saved by grace. But it's even more than that. Responding to Jesus Christ and becoming "born again" is when we are given citizenship into the kingdom of God. This not only affects where we have our eternal home, but it affects how we live this life in the here and now. The kingdom of God is transformative.

> *We are the beautiful, beloved daughters of a perfect and powerful King.*

The kingdom of God is perfected love and power, a realm of indescribable beauty. Because King Jesus is beauty, love, perfection, and power, and we belong to Him, we are the beautiful, beloved daughters of a perfect and powerful King. By His grace alone, that is who we are. It may not always be how we see ourselves or reflected in how we live, but it *is* our spiritual identity nonetheless. The more we understand and embrace this undeserved identity, the more glory and honor we will bring to our King. Our Father.

One of my favorite years of my life was 1995. It was the year I had the joy of planning my wedding and getting married. I realize that not everyone considers planning a wedding to be a joy. I get that. But for me, it *was* pure joy. Every. Single. Moment. I never felt stressed out. Rather, I felt like a kid in a candy shop for months on end.

Now, I'm a planner and organizer by nature, so I'm sure that helped. But what I really loved was selecting and designing every detail to create the exact look and mood that I had been imagining for my wedding most of my life. And boy, did I have an intense imagination! One of those design details included a crown.

Yes. I said a crown.

Now I realize that one person's tastes, preferences, and styles can be extremely different from another's. Some people like things simple or small. Some people like offbeat or avant-garde. Some people like whatever the latest trend is. And some really don't care at all.

And then there are those like me who love *big*, dramatic, glamorous affairs. I have always been that way, and I am 100 percent unapologetic for it. Even when it's not totally "on trend," I'm the glamour girl. You can keep your reclaimed wood, pale-neutral tones, wheat stalks and sunflowers, restored barn doors and Mason jars. Give me the Palace of Versailles!

So as you can probably imagine by now, my wedding was something out of a Disney fairy tale. I'm sure it made some people want to barf, but not me! The dress I chose was very formal and princess-like, and I'm telling you, it weighed more than me (and I have never been considered "petite"!). Naturally, I needed a veil and tiara to compliment my princess gown. Duh!

As for the veil, I set out to have one of the longest "veil trains" you have ever seen. I'm not referring to the train on my gown. This was a train on my *veil*, and it extended *past* the train on my gown. It was a light and airy design of thirty yards of tulle, with hand-glued Swarovski crystals scattered about to catch the light just right. I hand-glued each one myself. The veil was so long that it needed to be lifted and carried by four of my flower girls so it didn't get stuck on the carpet.

Yes, I said *four* of my flower girls. There were thirteen children in total. Twenty-four in the bridal party and eight candle-lighters. It was an evening wedding in a big sanctuary, and there were a lot of candles! And in the old days, you actually had people dressed up, formally lighting the candles, with these fancy, long, curved, gold contraptions, at the beginning of the ceremony.

The veil needed to be attached to something on my head, of course. Now most women in the '80s and '90s chose a delicate headpiece of some sort. Those were very popular. Especially the ones that formed a V shape on your forehead.

My mother and I went shopping for tiaras one day. (If you are unfamiliar, tiaras are usually U-shaped with the focal point being front and center, not a continuous circle like a crown.) I was browsing among the generous selection of beautiful tiaras when I noticed up on a top shelf something even more magnificent. Yep, you guessed it, *a crown!*

A full-on, full circle, gold-and-rhinestone-studded, four-inch tall crown! My eyes lit up, and I pointed, "I have got to try *that* one on!" I'm pretty sure my mom just laughed, as this came as no surprise to her! I tried it on and knew instantly that it was "the one." It perfectly fit my larger-than-average-sized head. I'm not implying that I have a "big head" metaphorically. No, I literally have a big head! So this substantial crown was the perfect accessory for my heavy, sequined, regal gown and extra-long veil.

At this point in my story, I would just like to say I realize that I could be creating the impression that I was spoiled or an attention seeker. All I can say is I really wasn't. There *was* a limit to how much money could be spent, especially by today's standards. I was extremely grateful to be able to create the wedding of my dreams, and I knew it was a privilege. It wasn't about an unhealthy need for attention either. I just genuinely love styles and looks that are more glamorous. They make my heart happy.

Another reason I chose to have a large wedding is that my parents had been in church ministry at the same large church for the majority of their lives. I was blessed to have been raised with *so* many "family friends" that we considered "our family."

A large wedding allowed my family to include the vast number of special people we had done life with for so many years. It was important to me and my parents to include as many of those friends and family as we could. Having a vast sea of familiar faces on one of the most important days of my life meant everything to me.

I remember that day so well. For me, it was beautiful in every way. Not just in the way the creative design and planning came together but also in the fact that I had chosen a man with a beautiful heart to be my husband. I want to make it clear that I am incredibly grateful for the life I have been given.

I am a well-loved daughter of wonderful parents. I am a well-loved friend by so many lovely friends. And on that day in 1995, not only did I feel like a very "lovely bride," but I was also a bride who was very loved. And you know what else? I was a beloved daughter of a King. I still am. I may not have been fully familiar with that terminology and all that it meant then, but nonetheless, it was true.

When I consider that it was a *crown* that I chose to put on my head for that most splendid day, it holds such great significance for me. I *love* that *I chose to wear a crown*. I look back on it as a prophetic moment in my life. It pointed to a time when I would actually *live aware of my identity as a daughter of the King*. It stands as a picture of who I am and who every woman is who has made Jesus the Lord of her life.

Regardless of the life you had growing up or the life you have now, regardless of the difficult or unhappy circumstances you may be in, you need to know there is One whose love for you is so real and so powerful. God the Father sees you, and He knows you, and He created you on purpose! He longs for you to have an encounter with Him and His love because He knows it will change you from the inside out.

There is so much more of Him for you to discover and to know.

As a citizen of the kingdom of God, it's imperative to realize that living fully empowered as a woman has *nothing* to do with *earning* your identity and *striving* for significance. It has *nothing* to do with *fighting* for your rights, recognition, or respect. Instead, it has everything to do with your royal identity as a daughter of the King! And daughters of kings have crowns. I may be speaking metaphorically here, but one day the Bible says we will be given a crown that is not metaphorical.

Second Timothy 4:8 (CSB) states, "There is reserved for me a *crown* of righteousness, which the Lord, the righteous judge, will give to me on that day."

And we read in Revelation 4:10 about the twenty-four elders in heaven who fall down at the throne of God, casting their crowns before Him in worship. Most biblical scholars agree that we, too, will one day cast our crowns before the King. The very crowns He gave to us.

I remember, as a child, on Sunday mornings, walking with my dad from the church parking lot to the outside halls of our Sunday school rooms. When we came near my Sunday school room, my dad would pull some loose change from his pocket and hand it to me. That was my offering money. I loved to put that money in the miniature white plastic chapel that was designed just for children's offerings as a slit in the top of the roof where you would put your coins.

I learned early on the joy of giving. But the money wasn't even mine. I didn't have my own money, so my dad gave me what I needed for that act of worship. It's the very same thing with the crowns we will one day receive from our Father God. *He* provides for us that which we don't have in order to worship Him in the way He deserves. And I know that act of worship in heaven will be one of immense pleasure and joy. What a good, good Father we have.

One of the biggest privileges and blessings of my own life is being loved by a good, good earthly father. Not everyone can say that. If there's one thing I'm keenly aware of, it's that life is certainly not fair. So much of my understanding of God has been shaped in a positive way because of my experience with a kind and loving earthly dad. The older I get, the more I realize just how precious a gift it was to be raised by a mother and father who loved me unconditionally, sacrificially, and with the utmost devotion. My family wasn't perfect by any means, but I was a well-loved and cared-for child, and that holds profound importance in my security and development as a child, all the way into adulthood. It's actually quite humbling to take in the fact that what I was able to experience growing up is certainly not the experience of so many others. I'm grateful. Really really grateful.

Regardless of the inequity in people's experiences with their earthly parents, and particularly with their earthly father, everyone has the opportunity to become a child of the most perfect Father they could ever imagine. Yet He isn't a product of the imagination. He is a real, living Creator and King. He is God with a capital G, and He is absolutely and only good. His love is incomprehensible, really, but we can experience His love in great measure just the same. His faithfulness and care are unparalleled, and yet, no matter who we are, we can receive them.

We are daughters of the King, and when we live *from* that royal identity, we soon discover that there is *so* much more for us than fighting and striving our way through life. So much more for us than living like orphans, abandoned into forced self-reliance. Untrusting, afraid, undernourished, defensive, insecure, and living in continuous lack. That is not how we have been designed to live and exist in this world. That is not the life we were created for.

However, we do have an enemy who will do everything he can to tell us otherwise. Our own earthly experiences with parents who have shaped our understanding of God in a negative and distorted way can stand as a huge roadblock in our understanding and perception of God the Father. But on the other side of the lies and the roadblocks stands the truth of who God really is and how much you are really loved.

Loved in perfection by the only One who is absolutely perfect.

That's why it is time to discover the power, the beauty, and the freedom of living in our royal identity. It's time to wear the crown.

CHAPTER 2:
Live Like Royalty

Royalty is my identity. Servanthood is my
assignment. Intimacy with God is my life source.

— Bill Johnson

When you gave your life to Christ, you were adopted into the royal family of God and given the name "daughter" for all eternity. God has made you His legal heir, and "orphan" is no longer your name because you are a "child of the King." That is a kind of empowerment you will never find through other women or men because the earth cannot give us what it does not possess.

So why is it that our lives too often do not reflect this reality? Many live lost, searching for meaning and purpose. Many live hungry, searching for validation and recognition. Many live anxious, searching for peace and rest.

When we live our lives in our own strength, according to our own wills, and with our own agenda, we end up living far below the potential we were created with. But when we live our life deeply connected to the Life-Giver, we will be infused with a kind of power the world does not know and a kind of beauty the world cannot display. It will be a life that goes beyond the ordinary and finds the extraordinary type of empowerment of a person not only *in whom* the Holy Spirit resides but *on whom* the Holy Spirit longs to rest.

We are all given the precious gift of the Holy Spirit at salvation. But there are certain realities to living in the *fullness* of the power of the Holy Spirit that require consistent, intentional pursuit and humble surrender. The Spirit of God lives in us always. But the Spirit of God is looking for people *on* whom He can rest in power and anointing.

Jesus said in Matthew 5:6 that those who hunger and thirst after righteousness will be blessed by being filled up with all they hunger and thirst for. God Himself *is* righteousness, and when we hunger and thirst after *Him*, we will find the blessing of living a life that is full and filled. A life fulfilled.

It is *this* kind of life that testifies to our royal identity and reveals who our Father is and what His kingdom is like. It's *this* kind of life that reflects the very nature of God. And it is *this* kind of life where peace is superior to anxiety. Joy is superior to grief and sadness. Hope is superior to discouragement. And trust is superior to doubt. Meaning this… peace, joy, hope, and trust are available to us without measure, and they are powerful tools in overcoming anxiety, grief, sadness, discouragement, and doubt.

I'm not talking about a life free from hard realities and difficult circumstances. Or a life free from suffering, pain, or sorrow. Those things exist! They are real. And for some people, they exist in greater measure because life isn't fair. But they do *not* have to have the last word. And they do not have to hold us hostage. We are meant to live a life where the fruit of righteousness flows from an abundance of the goodness of God that our hearts have encountered in a tangible way.

> *We are meant to live a life where the fruit of righteousness flows from an abundance of the goodness of God that our hearts have encountered in a tangible way.*

One description of the kingdom of God is found in Romans 14:17 (CSB): "The Kingdom of God is Righteousness, Peace and Joy in the Holy Spirit." So ask yourself this… when others see me, do they find a *righteousness* that has no "self" in it? Do they feel the presence of a *peace* that they don't quite understand? And when others encounter me, do they come face to face with a type of resilient *joy* they have never known?

These are the questions I have been asking myself because if I have been promised participation in the divine nature of God, who is love, then others *must* be able to see and sense a different kind of love in me, a love whose nature is divine.

It is our great privilege and honor and joy to reveal the heart of the Father and the goodness of God to everyone around us.

I don't think I really understood this for most of my life as a believer. I was familiar with the expectation that I needed to be a good witness for God. But that somehow translated to "Don't do anything that would make God look bad or cause Him to be disappointed in you." I think this is how many people in the body of Christ view their responsibility of being a "good Christian."

Once I began to really understand the foundational truth of just how good God is and that He is a good Father with a heart of indescribable love for all people and for *me*, I discovered my purpose in representing Him to the world or *re*-presenting Him. The focus then moved from the idea of "being on your best behavior" to something far deeper and far more impactful. It's all about knowing His heart of love and goodness toward me and then expressing His heart and goodness for others in a myriad of creative and enjoyable ways. Remember Jesus said, His "yoke is *easy*" and His "burden is *light*" (Matthew 11:30).

Living as a reflection of God's love and goodness is true, authentic beauty that radiates from the inside out. It brings joy and life to the receiver and the giver. It's not a list of rules and regulations to which we can never measure up, weighing us down with guilt and shame. And it's not pressure! If that has been your primary experience or understanding of how this life with Christ works, then I have really good news for you. You're wrong.

When I was little, I went to Sunday school. I don't mean casually or occasionally. I mean every single Sunday of my entire life. Okay, that may be a little dramatic but pretty much true. I remember a song we would sing in fourth grade Sunday school. It was my favorite song.

The plastic chairs were lined up in three or four nice rows. And if my Sunday dress wasn't of the long variety, the back of my thighs would stick to the plastic when it was warm. There were no air conditioners in those old Sunday school rooms. But there was a piano and a flannelgraph board.

Just saying the words "flannelgraph board" ages me tremendously. For those of you not familiar with this archaic term, it is basically a felt-covered board that paper figures of Jesus and Bible people and Bible scenery would stick to. It would serve as a visual for whichever story the teaching was telling. I couldn't wait until I was an old Sunday school teacher and could use that flannelgraph board when I told the stories. #goals.

Anyway, as I was saying, there was a piano. And it was old too. And the man sitting on the piano bench plunking out the notes in a frenetic fashion each week was also old. But I liked him, and the piano, and the song. I still remember all the words.

> He owns the cattle on a thousand hills. The wealth in every mine.
> He owns the rivers and the rock and rills [I think it was rills… but what's a rill?] The sun and stars that shine.
> Wonderful riches more than tongue can tell [And here comes my favorite part…]
> *He is my father so they're mine as well!*

Oh, I would sing that last line like I was "Annie" in Daddy Warbuck's grand entryway! I reveled in the thought of possessing wealth and wonderful riches, even if it were cows and hills and rocks and rills. Now you might say that the glee I had while singing this song points to a selfish, materialistic propensity in my little fourth-grade self. And maybe that was in there somewhere. But here's what I really think... the Spirit of God in my little heart recognized a deep and wonderful truth: "He is my Father, and everything that is His is mine."

The love of the Father is mine. The treasures of the kingdom are mine. Not because I'm good or because I earned them. Not because I figured out how to sin less or loved God better than someone else. The "wonderful riches" are mine because I am *His*. Period. End of sentence.

Which reminds me of another Sunday school song...

"I'm my beloved's and He is mine. His banner
over me is love."

I didn't quite understand the beauty of those words in the fourth grade, but I do now. In fourth grade, what I really liked about that song was the "motions." What we referred to as the "motions" way back in the old days is what now might be called "choreography." A word with far more flair and excitement. But that was probably a bit too secular-sounding for Sunday school. We didn't dance, mind you. We did all sorts of things with our arms, and we called those "the motions."

Circling back to the point...

Knowing the heart of the Father for us and for the world around us, *really knowing* His goodness and His love experientially, not just intellectually, is something we do not want to live without. And guess what? The world doesn't want to live without it either; it just doesn't know that yet. Sadly, some of you haven't yet known or understood the depths of God's love and goodness. But it's not too late. There is still time for you to know God in ways you have never known Him. There is still time for you to realize your "royal" potential and purpose as the hands, feet, and mouth of Jesus.

The world is in agony. You can feel it and see it. Sometimes, its ugliness is so pervasive, and it reflects the wretchedness of the enemy, who always stands in direct opposition to the beauty of God. So many people search desperately for love and have no idea who He really is. They are confused and think themselves to be enlightened. They are deceived and consider themselves to be wise. They are starving and believe themselves to be full.

The world *needs* a *victorious* church! A people of peace, joy, hope, and love amid chaos, sorrow, and destruction. A people of strength whose power is rooted in faith and flows from love. We must be a picture of what's possible in a world fraught with impossibility. A wise pastor said, "We always reflect the nature of the realm we are most aware of." Read that again. I'll wait.

Are we going to live more aware of the kingdoms of this earth or the kingdom of heaven, the kingdom of our citizenship? Jesus preached the kingdom, and He *lived* the kingdom, and He said, "The kingdom of heaven is at hand." It was not a kingdom of "flesh and blood," which the Jewish people were expecting. It was an unseen heavenly kingdom, an unseen realm that could only be seen through the Spirit of Truth. Jesus taught that the kingdom of heaven looks nothing like the kingdoms of the earth.

We will always reflect the kingdom from which *we* operate! We must *know* and *understand* that there is a vast difference!

And we are not living our best lives when we look and sound and think like everyone else around us. Living unaware of the kingdom of God. When we live awake and present to the things that are "not of this world," we live with a deep spiritual awareness of the Holy Spirit, who is alive in us. What we have been given in Christ and what is available to us because of God's infinite grace, mercy, and love is staggering when we really take it in.

That is why I no longer desire to live a powerless life of ho-hum Christianity. It doesn't do me any good, and it doesn't do anyone else any good. And dare I say that living far beneath the life I have been called and equipped to live is an insult to the cross, and it's an insult to the King.

I received Christ at the young age of five years old. My favorite grandma led me through the process of "asking Jesus into my heart." I remember it well. I had been caught lying and was very grieved by it. My grandma shared with me how Jesus forgives us and how He wants to live in us to make us more like Him because He loves us. That experience holds great significance, and I will never discount that moment of salvation. But it took me many years to get more serious about my faith. It was a slow process of transformation, complete with ups, downs, ins, and outs. I have walked with Jesus for many years now, but only in my later years has my understanding of God, His kingdom, and how it operates expanded to the point where I now have begun to live differently. To think differently. To respond differently.

Accessing the power and the authority I carry because of my royal identity in Christ is the source of my ability to live a life of empowerment in the Holy Spirit. This has brought me to new levels of freedom, expectation, and faith, knowing I have the power of heaven backing me up!

Jesus perfectly modeled for us the life we are called to live. And then He sent His Spirit to equip us with everything we will ever need to walk in His footsteps.

You and I, we are daughters of the King and heirs of His kingdom. We are royalty. So let's live like it.

CHAPTER 3:
Don't Believe Everything You Think

How we think not only affects our own spirit, soul and body, but also people around us.

— Dr. Caroline Leaf

So where do we start? How do we begin to live with more spiritual awareness and see the fruit of living with a kingdom mindset? The wise instruction of Romans 12:2 (KJV) is an excellent place to begin. It says, "Be not conformed to this world, but be ye transformed by the renewing of your mind."

So much of changing our lives begins with changing our minds, or rather our mindsets, our belief structures, our inner narrative and dialogue. It's literally changing how we think. Because changing the way we think or what we are thinking has a direct effect on the way we feel, respond, react, or act in life and relationships.

Not all thoughts are accurate, healthy, reasonable, justified, helpful, or productive. Many thoughts are, in fact, distorted, hostile, shaming, cynical, accusatory, and ungrateful. And not just thoughts about others, but thoughts about ourselves. Our inner dialogue holds an immense amount of power and influence over us and the environments we create.

Let's face it — so many people live unaware of all the junk going on in their minds. It's been there for so long, and it feels so normal that it goes largely undetected. Yet, the effects of our thoughts and mindsets are *huge!* Don't ever underestimate that. *And don't believe everything you think!*

Christian cognitive neuroscientist Dr. Caroline Leaf has shed so much light on this subject in such a practical way. Her research and insight perfectly marry science and Scripture. This should come as no surprise since without God there would be no "science." In her book *Switch on Your Brain*, she writes, "Our choices — the natural consequences of thoughts and imagination — get under the skin of our DNA and can turn certain genes on and off, changing the structure of the neurons in our brain. Our minds are amazing creations."

We've all heard the term "mindfulness." I believe mindfulness is "checking our thoughts at the door." I like to think of it this way: our minds need "security checkpoints" where the toxic thoughts are detained and scrutinized. The ones that don't line up with "truth" get thrown out.

For Christ followers, it can be described as taking our thoughts captive and making them obedient to Christ (2 Corinthians 10:5). I'm sure most of you are familiar with that verse but may have not fully understood what it meant in a practical way. Maybe we'll start with what it doesn't mean, which is being super-duper religious and only thinking about religious things.

What it does mean, however, is filtering out the thoughts that are deceptively toxic for us and those around us. The ones that are inherently opposed to the nature of God. The ones that aren't "truth."

Dr. Caroline explains it this way, "When you objectively observe your own thinking with the view to capturing rogue thoughts, you in effect direct your own attention to stop the negative impact and rewire healthy new circuits into your brain."

I find it fascinating that a spiritual directive or practice given to us in the Scriptures, such as "taking our thoughts captive and making them obedient to Christ," has not only spiritual implications but actual physiological and emotional benefits as well. We are holistic creations — mind, body, soul, and spirit.

Knowing which thoughts are not founded in biblical truth presents us with one of the most important keys in renewing our minds: *knowing the Scriptures*. The more truth and promises of God's Word we get into our hearts and minds, the less we will be battered and confused by all the thoughts that are opposed to the truth. The thoughts that mislead, confuse, convolute, deceive, mistreat, and ultimately destroy.

> *The more truth and promises of God's Word we get into our hearts and minds, the less we will be battered and confused by all the thoughts that are opposed to the truth.*

I used to feel like reading my Bible was… well, to be super honest, really boring. Because I really didn't know where to start, I would flip through it and randomly read "whatever" and find my mind would wander. Or I would read something I didn't understand or even like. It was a struggle for a while. And for a lot of my young adult life, it was nonexistent.

I grew up in church, and I attended a Christian school. I had a lot of Bible exposure, and for that I am really grateful. But the one thing that you might say was not an advantage was that the Bible became more like a textbook to me. And for five days of the week, it was quite literally a textbook. I would carry it through my high school hallways, along with my math book, my English book, my history book… see where I'm going with this?

I hated to study. I hated it! I hated tests and homework and anything that had to do with traditional subjects and traditional education. Now if they had offered "make-up artistry" or "event planning" as classes, I would have been all in. And probably valedictorian. But they didn't.

When it came to spiritual things, I guess I was your average 1980s Christian-raised teenager. I would pore over every word and lyric on my Amy Grant LP but not read Romans unless I had to. I would enjoy going to midweek church, but mainly to see my friends and do fun drama stuff for the youth group. But I wasn't really crazy about sharing something God had been "showing me" with a small group. I didn't have that kind of spiritual depth. I was saved. I had asked Jesus in my heart as a little girl, and that meant something. I do believe that.

Yet, I have wondered sometimes if being so immersed in a Christian culture somehow almost inoculated me against a deep, personal encounter or revelation of the tangible and transformative love of God. Don't get me wrong — I knew God loved me. But it was what we church folk like to refer to as "head knowledge." I had heard it my whole life. And that is pretty wonderful! I'm not criticizing, so please hear my heart on that. I'm only recognizing the possibility of something becoming so *over*familiar that you have difficulty realizing its value or being deeply moved by it.

Somehow, I also assumed God was disappointed and subsequently disinterested in me because I wasn't a "picture-perfect" Christian (whatever that is). I wasn't a bad Christian like some of my friends might have been unfortunately labeled. But I wasn't a great one either. Like the ones who were comfortable praying out loud or loved reading their Bibles! Let's be real. I was a compliant pew-sitter who thought sermons were very boring and couldn't wait for church to be over.

There was a point in my life right before I met my husband when the Holy Spirit broke through just enough for me to get a glimpse of where my spiritual life really was. And it was kind of pathetic. Not nonexistent but really suffering from paralysis. Oh yes, I was still going to church, and I actually loved going to church in my college and young adult years. I had great friends who wanted to follow Jesus. I was super involved in music and drama ministry. I loved God and being a part of a church family, but my *personal relationship* with the Lord was kind of shallow. I think perhaps this may describe more people in the body of Christ than we realize.

The great thing about authentically hearing the Holy Spirit is that He's never the One responsible for making you feel guilty. Guilt is not the language He speaks. Neither is shame. And when He broke through to me, I didn't feel guilty. I felt conviction. However, many misunderstand "conviction" and believe it to be something it's not.

The dictionary definition of "conviction" is a "guilty verdict" or a "firmly held belief." That's not what biblical conviction means. You see, when the Holy Spirit is correcting us through conviction, He is not declaring a guilty verdict over us. He is redirecting us, and there is an underlying passion to it, but it is gentle and kind. I would say that the conviction of the Holy Spirit is "love with an edge."

In that moment, I actually felt known. And well… loved. The voice of the Spirit, who was surely in me, communicated to my heart that I was made for more. That I was missing out on something divinely beautiful and fulfilling. He spoke in such a way that His words gave me a picture of God knowing how much *more* my life could be about and Him wanting *me* to know it too. It wasn't a "shame on you"; it was more like "Come take My hand and step out into new territory. Let Me show you what you're missing. I hold in My hands the better thing." I responded to *that*, and my life with Jesus began to grow.

There was a significant shift in my relationship with the Lord. But it still took time to grow into what it looks like today. There were markers along the way, however, and those times stand out to me as moments of fresh discovery or experience. I began to enjoy my Bible more. I can't say I fell hard and fast in love with God's Word, but it did begin to speak to me in ways it hadn't before. And then, about fifteen years ago or so, I really got interested in studying the Scriptures. It took on new life and new meaning. I didn't follow a plan or Bible study per se. I just started *really* reading. Looking for the deeper meanings and hidden treasures.

I am convinced that there is not "one right way" to approach diving into God's Word. I think we discover what works for us. The way we approach Scripture will reflect our own unique personality and approach to learning. If you're in the beginning stages of discovering the awesomeness of the Bible, I would encourage you to just dive in and try different things. And always ask the Holy Spirit to speak to you and reveal truths to you. I promise He will.

A kingdom mindset begins when we discover the absolute beauty of the Bible. It's a living, breathing thing. It's the very breath of God written down as a multilayered, overarching love story between Him and us. We desperately need its wisdom and truth as we step into our God-given authority and take control over our minds.

If that sounds daunting… well, it can be when we don't invite the Holy Spirit to be our guide.

Jesus told His followers that "when the Spirit of Truth comes he will guide you into all truth…. because He will take from what is mine and declare it to you. Everything the Father has is mine" (John 16:13–15, CSB).

That is actually saying that everything the Father gives Jesus is given to us through the Holy Spirit! Utterly amazing!

According to 1 Corinthians 2:16–17, those who live by the Spirit have the mind of Christ. Talk about a kingdom treasure!

Without the Spirit of Truth, who is the Holy Spirit, it's awfully hard to not believe everything we think. A kingdom mindset requires that I set my mind on things above, not earthly things (Colossians 3:2).

We renew our minds with *truth*. And Jesus is that truth. The words on the pages are *truth*; they are promises, wise counsel, and godly instruction. They are even examples of what *not* to do or how *not* to think!

Read through the Old Testament, and you'll read plenty of stories about people who did horrible things and made horrible choices. People like us who believed completely wrong things and believed the wrong gods. Most of these accounts are obvious, but some are not.

Just look at the psalms. David was so heart-wrenchingly honest with his feelings. He cried out to God unfiltered. He had real enemies and threats coming against him and felt his anxiety and sorrows so deeply. He could easily identify what he *felt*, but he seemed to have spent more time rejoicing and declaring what he *knew* to be the truth!

Psalm 10 begins with David saying, "Lord, why do you stand so far away? Why do you hide in times of trouble?" (v. 1, CSB). Have we not all *felt* that way at some point in our lives? Yes, in our human experience, we have known this to be "true." But it is not *truth*. The truth is found in verses 17–18 (CSB), "Lord you have heard the desire of the humble; you will strengthen their hearts. You will listen carefully, doing justice for the fatherless and oppressed."

Psalm 13 begins similarly, "How long, Lord? Will you forget me forever? How long will you hide your face from me?" (v. 1, CSB). And the chapter closes with this declaration of faith, "But I have trusted in your faithful love; my heart will rejoice in your deliverance. I will sing to the Lord because He has treated me generously" (CSB).

When I begin to see myself and others through the lens of Scripture and begin to see my circumstances, whether good or bad, with the eyes of a well-loved daughter of the King, I am then learning how to renew my mind and align it with the truth of the Word.

My mind becomes the filter through which damaging thoughts get trapped and lies get exposed. The enemy loves to use our minds to get at us. So often, we view him as a little red devil who tempts us to do, say, or think horrible things. Unfortunately, he's more clever, crafty, and subtle than that. He disguises himself in ways that allow him to deceive us more prolifically if we let him. In fact, the Bible says he masquerades as "an angel of light" (2 Corinthians 11:14). I'm pretty sure it's his favorite costume.

If he can get us to believe things in our minds, he can go a long way with his destructive nature in our lives. Not only in just *believing things that aren't truth* but also in *doubting the things that are truth!* That's a signature tactic with him. It's the one he used in the garden. He asked Adam, "Did God *really* say... ?" and the rest is history. At the risk of oversimplification, we really have two choices regarding our beliefs. To believe the words of God or to believe the words of the enemy. And what we choose makes all the difference in the world.

It's time to stop believing everything we think, start renewing our minds, and be amazed at the transformation we will experience.

CHAPTER 4:
Learn a New Language

Language is the dress of thought.

— Samuel Johnson

When I was in tenth grade, I had to take Spanish. Man, I hated Spanish class, but I had the sweetest Spanish teacher. I wish I could remember his name. I felt really bad for the guy having me in his class because I was pretty much a linguistic idiot. Honestly, I don't suffer from low self-esteem, as much as that last statement may indicate. I really didn't care if I was good at Spanish or not. I just didn't want to see Mr. "Sweet Spanish Teacher" work so hard with me to no avail. I'm pretty sure he just "cooked the books" to give me a D on my report card, so we could both just call it a day.

For some of us, learning a new language is hard. Really hard. But a whole new world opens up to us when we do. It's the same in the kingdom of God.

The language of God's truth unleashes the power of the kingdom, which will lead to transformation. Our words reveal more than most of us realize. They reveal our beliefs, and our beliefs are usually the problem. Our deeply embedded beliefs influence our thoughts, and our thoughts shape our words. Part of surrendering our lives to Christ is surrendering our beliefs as well. The faulty ones: the ones that do not align with truth.

For instance, you may feel defeated. You may feel hopeless. You may feel abandoned.

And that may be "true"… but it's not "the truth." Because in Christ, you are *not* defeated, you are *not* hopeless, and you are *not* abandoned.

What we could often define as *"true"* in our lives is not the same thing as what is ultimately *"true"* according to God's truth. Understanding this seemingly small distinction has the power to yield unbelievably transformative results.

I can be facing the uncertainties of life that bring anxiety and fear or cause doubt and discouragement, but when I *choose* to look up and lock eyes with my good, good Father and say the words found in Psalm 91:2 (NIV), "I will say of the Lord, HE is my refuge and my fortress; my God in Him I will trust!" those become the words of life and truth that sustain me and strengthen me.

There is so much freedom to be found when our lives are transformed by the renewing of our minds. Once we integrate a lifestyle of renewing our minds with the truth, we will find ourselves learning a new language: the language of heaven.

Words hold power. Proverbs 18:21 tells us that "the power of life and death is in the tongue." That's a really profound truth. And Proverbs 12:14 (NIV) says, "From the fruit of their lips people are filled with good things." According to this verse, it's possible that what comes into our mind, soul, and spirit can be the result of what comes out of our mouths.

There is so much freedom to be found when our lives are transformed by the renewing of our minds. Once we integrate a lifestyle of renewing our minds with the truth, we will find ourselves learning a new language: the language of heaven.

When we choose to speak words of life, like gratitude and thanksgiving, faith and trust, encouragement and love, we fill ourselves with good things. Words often become declarations over our lives and the lives of others. Declarations are, in essence, a type of faith statement about what is true. But so many live unaware of this reality. What we say matters. It makes all the difference.

The enemy, Satan, is constantly setting traps in hopes of ensnaring us. And the trap of "words" is a big one with him. He knows just how powerful words are and that speaking his language does damage.

The Bible calls him "the father of lies." It's the language of death, and he speaks that language fluently. Not one single word can be trusted because every word is always in direct opposition to the Father. Jesus said that He only spoke what the *Father* was saying; He lived in perfect alignment with heaven's language.

Speaking in opposition to the Father will always be the voice of the enemy.

Lies oppress us and are many times difficult to identify if we're not in the habit of doing so. Lies we have come to believe over time begin to blend into the fabric of our consciousness so well that they can be easily missed. To gain expertise in identifying lies we believe, we must become experts at knowing the truth.

The truth of God's nature, His Word, His promises, and the truth of who we are in Him and to Him are the very things we must so acutely attune ourselves to. When we do, the very thoughts, attitudes, and beliefs that are misaligned with the truth are then more easily recognized and identified. To focus our attention on Him and immerse ourselves in the Word can be our opportunity to adjust our perspective and come back into alignment.

The truth is what sets us free. But it's not just any truth or our own version of truth. Authentic, absolute truth is not whatever we decide it to be. Rather, transforming, life-giving truth is only found in Jesus, who is the "Word."

John 1:1 (NIV) begins with this: "In the beginning was the Word and the Word was with God and the Word was God." What a beautiful way John described His Master, Jesus of Nazareth. Jesus said, "If you continue in my Word, you are truly my disciples, then you will know the truth, and the truth will set you free" (John 8:31–32, RSV).

Remember the enemy often uses subtle tactics, and he certainly does this as he seeks to have influence over us, realizing the importance and the power of our words. It's easier to be aware of words that stand out as evil. But how about the less evil words? For instance, it's not just blatant words of hate or perversion, outright lies or brutal slander. It's the more subtle words of doubt, unbelief, negativity, criticism, complaint, and hopelessness that can be just as destructive.

We don't have to be in total denial of the realities we feel or face to speak heaven's language of truth. I'm not suggesting we just "pretend" everything is better or different from what it actually is. The familiar words of Joel 3:10 (KJV) say, "Let the weak say, 'I am strong.'"

Author and speaker Steve Backlund points out that this verse doesn't tell us to say, "I'm not weak," or deny our weakness but to declare that we are strong. And why? Because *in* Christ, we find our strength. He lends us His strength. Just like the apostle Paul says in 2 Corinthians 12:9 (NIV), "My grace is sufficient for you, for my power is perfected in weakness." Steve puts it this way, "Our experience will catch up to our beliefs and the gap time is called faith. It's really hard to change your life without changing the way you think."

Viewing every circumstance and challenge in light of the greatness of our God is living with His promises and His goodness in *full* view. It is His love and His power, over us and in us, that empowers us to live as overcomers! Jesus said, "In this world you will have trouble, but take heart, I have overcome the world!" (John 16:33, NIV).

Heavy hearts weighed down by sorrow, minds filled with doubt and unbelief, spirits laden with criticism and negativity, circumstances that scream hopelessness, and spoken words of complaint are all invitations. Invitations to check our beliefs, identify the lies, weigh our words, and replace them with truth.

Then we may speak the language of heaven, regardless of what we may see or feel. And *this* is transformation.

A very common form of harmful speech is complaining. We've all done it, we all do it, but many are habitual complainers. The root of complaint is fear and unbelief. There is a thread that connects them to one another. Pastor Bill Johnson has these wise insights about complaining:

> Perspective is lost in complaining; it distorts our view of reality and clouds our vision. Complaining causes us to move in the momentum of unbelief that cancels our God-given ability to simply trust Him. Complaining is the language of fear and unbelief. It comes out of the heart that has a "Lordship" issue. Where the Lordship of Jesus is being compromised, complaining will be the evidence. Nobody complains who sees God's role in the middle of their situation. The complaint happens when we've lost sight of who He is and where He is.

When it comes to feeling justified in our complaints, he has this to say: "All you have to do is remove the promises and the presence of God out of the equation to be legalized in your complaining."

There's just no way around it. Complaining is toxic. It's the language of death. I don't mean to sound over dramatic, but *nothing* good results from complaining. It not only reveals the fear and unbelief in our hearts, but complaining takes us deeper into misery and loss of perspective and further away from the promise and purpose we were designed for.

The Israelites wandered around in the wilderness for forty years, not because it took that long to get to the promised land. It was a relatively short distance away. Simply stated, it was their chronic complaining and grumbling against Moses and God, rooted and manifested in unbelief, that kept them out of their promised land (Numbers 14). It would behoove us greatly to learn from their experience.

What we think and how we think, what we believe and how we believe, what we speak and how we speak greatly affects the fruit of our lives.

When it comes to harmful speech, here's another extremely common and toxic practice of our culture. Anxious words of worry!

These kinds of words can be even *more* deceiving than other words rooted in lies because we see them as completely normal and justifiable. We can even view them as empathetic when we use them to express our fears or to connect with others. But they're not as reasonable as we'd like to think. Neither are they empathic.

Anxious words of worry have no nutritional value for our spirits and our minds. They don't nourish or encourage us. They don't build our faith or affirm our trust. Anxious words of worry drain us of life. And they are not any more helpful when offered up to others.

People don't need us to be worried and anxious and fearful on their behalf nearly as much as they need us to be filled with faith and hope on their behalf. *That* is what imparts strength and courage, not our worry. We are admonished in Scripture to *not* worry. Yet, somehow, we tend to gloss over that pointed instruction as if it were merely a nice suggestion. Worry has unfortunately become a necessity to most, and a perfectly reasonable one at that.

When we stop to really think about it, we've been conditioned to believe that we're expressing love when we're worried and anxious on someone's behalf. But we must be really careful with that type of thinking.

Worry is not the same thing as healthy empathy. Empathy says, "I see and feel how you're struggling or hurting, and I recognize how difficult it must be." Empathy is beautiful, especially when we *lead* with empathy, but do *not stop* there. Empathy can pave the way for hope to be received. And hope is offered when we speak words of truth and life. Those are the words that actually "bear one another's burdens" as we're instructed to do in Galatians 6:2. Those are the words that reflect the power of Jesus, who declared Himself to be "the way, the truth, and the life." Anxious worry and fear, in actuality, are counterfeit empathy that offers no solution or hope.

Philippians 4:6 (NKJV) begins with, "Be anxious for *nothing*." That's a huge exhortation.

In the absence of anxious worry, we will speak words of life, encouragement, and hope that are anchored in truth. Truth that originates from the kingdom of God. When we determine to renew our minds, we will find that it's a constant, intentional practice of relinquishing our worried words over to Jesus in exchange for hope-filled truth. The language of life.

And you know what happens when we replace our worry with words of truth and hope? We find peace. Worries are the weeds in our garden of peace. They will take over and choke out life. That is why they must be pulled up and thrown out. When we read "be anxious for nothing," it does not go on to say... "when there is nothing to feel anxious about." We all know far too well those moments are rare. We will always find things we could be worried or feel anxious about. But there's a better way!

Let's go on with Philippians 4:6–7 (CSB), "Don't worry about anything, but in everything through prayer and petition with thanksgiving, present your requests to God. And the peace of God which surpasses all understanding, will guard your hearts and minds in Christ Jesus."

Again, Bill Johnson makes a profound observation when he says, "Worry replaces worship." The opposite is true as well. Worship replaces worry. We cannot be worried and in worship at the same time. And nothing will realign your spirit and your mind more than focused worship for Jesus and His love.

Other than reading Scripture verses that build up my faith, bring me hope, and give me peace, for me "worship" is very often singing songs that declare the truth of Scripture. I'll turn up the tunes and go for a drive or clean the bathroom. I'm serious — the acoustics are great, and I forget all about the fact that I'm cleaning the bathroom!

For you, it may be something different. Worship can be creative and reflect our uniqueness. But worship will do more for putting a heart at ease and a mind at peace than anything else.

In John 6:63 (NIV), Jesus said to the crowd at Capernaum, "The words that I have spoken to you — they are full of the Spirit and of life."

I want to be a person who speaks words that are "full of the Spirit and of life," *especially* when life is difficult and challenges arise. When things look hopeless and dire. When I'm afraid or discouraged. When I'm confused and don't understand. These are the precise moments I need to speak with more intentionality than ever! My words have the power to not only renew *my* mind and change *my* perspective but to also help change someone else's perspective as well.

There are plenty of people, believers even, who have never realized the healing power of speaking God's truth over a situation or over a life. And when we integrate the practice of "renewing our minds" and "changing our language" into our own lives, we can then introduce others to a new way of facing life's challenges. By living out what we believe about the power of the tongue, our words and our lives can become a testimony. Demonstrating what it looks like to live with a kingdom perspective, living from a place of victory, the place of peace and hope and joy, despite the circumstance.

This is a language that I am fully committed to learning, practicing, and becoming fluent in. The God who has asked me to learn a new language, the language of truth and of His Word, is faithful and willing to teach me and stick it out with me just like "Mr. Sweet Spanish Teacher." But with God, I won't fail. I may stumble and forget and need reminding. But I *will* see the fruit of a renewed mind and renewed tongue when I'm surrendered to Him and to the process.

The language of heaven is the language that flows from the heart of the Father. He sings over us His songs of deliverance. And He will quiet (our anxious hearts) with His love (Psalm 32:70 and Zephaniah 3:17).

I must turn my worry into worship — my doubts, fears, unbelief, hopelessness… all the things that drain the very life from me. When I turn all those things over to the Father in focused worship and cast my cares upon Him (1 Peter 5:7), I will then be speaking the language of my homeland. The language of heaven.

CHAPTER 5:
Raise a Hallelujah

A spirit of despair is no match for a garment of praise.

— Inspired by Isaiah 61:3

It was a Wednesday night church service when the lyrics to a familiar song I had sung many times before suddenly held fresh revelation and meaning. I love it when God does that. I stood there, arms raised, singing words that resonated so deeply with my heart and my mind. And my circumstances. The message of the song encourages the believer to never stop offering up praise and thanksgiving to the Lord, even and especially in difficult times. That, in fact, it's the most difficult of times that our sacrifice of praise and worship and thanksgiving is not only radical but most effective.

As I sang, the Spirit's message to my soul was this…

"Don't ever let the storm soften your voice or stop your song. You keep singing, and you sing it stronger and clearer. A storm is not the time to go soft or sing softly. It's the exact time to sing louder. Let your praises *roar!*"

Our God is the Lion of Judah, and the Lion doesn't back down when the enemy advances. The Lion lets out a roar and looks straight at the enemy with an authority and a power that declares, "You don't stand a chance!" The kingdom of God is superior. It is light. Darkness is always the inferior power. And the authority and power I carry, because of Jesus, comes from the kingdom of light.

Storms will come. Hardships will come. The attacks will come. But how I respond will make all the difference! Will I respond with declarations or words of fear or of victory? Will I respond with declarations or words of defeat or words of power?

You see, "Death and life are in the power of tongue" (Proverbs 18:21, CSB).

We often speak death over our life and speak life over our enemy when really we need to be speaking life in the storm and death to the enemy!

Satan roams around *like* a lion, seeking whom he may destroy. He's looking for an open door, an opportunity to kill, steal, and destroy. And he disguises himself as a lion because all he can do is play dress up and pretend!

There's only one Lion of Judah, and His name is Jesus Christ. The Lamb of God who takes away the sin of the world. The King sitting on the throne at the right hand of the Father. The beginning and the end. The final say. The author of life. The just judge. The King of kings and Lord of lords. The name above all names.

The fake lion is the king of the inferior kingdom of darkness. And the Scriptures say he must bow to the name that is above every other name: Jesus. So, if I'm walking in the power and the authority of the greater kingdom, the one of which I am a citizen, then why am I allowing the fake lion to intimidate me? To lie to me? To steal from me?

It is one thing to raise our hallelujahs in the celebration. It's quite another to raise our hallelujahs in the storm!

Which hallelujah do you think confounds and frustrates the enemy more? Which hallelujah takes my timidity and turns it into a mighty roar? It's the hallelujah raised in faith! It's the hallelujah that believes the One who says He is faithful will be faithful.

That hallelujah has the power to take what I feel and make it bow the knee to what I know! That hallelujah takes my burden and carries it so I don't have to. When I surrender my worry and doubt in my sacrifice of praise, I am strengthening myself in the Lord, just like David did. I'm also reminding the fake lion who he is and who I am. Courage rises up, my trust is made stronger, my peace becomes weightier, and my joy is made fuller.

When I raise my hallelujah with gratitude and thanksgiving for financial abundance and blessing, that's beautiful, pleasing, and good. But when I raise my hallelujah in gratitude and thanksgiving for a God who promises to meet my every need when there are only a few dollars left on the debit card, that's powerful and transformative! And that's pretty much the situation we were facing.

Those who live the "up-and-down," "come-and-go" lifestyle of the self-employed can really understand the sudden shifts and shimmies of income.

> *It is one thing to raise our hallelujahs in the celebration. It's quite another to raise our hallelujahs in the storm!*

It was so strange. We had just come through a season of some major financial breakthroughs and had implemented more spiritual practices, like sowing seeds, that took us to a whole new level of understanding, blessing, and stability as it pertained to money. Things were great. And then, well, things were weird. It was like someone had put a giant "cog in the wheel" or like a nasty "clog in the drain" or like a... well, I think you get the point.

You know when you're on your computer, and that annoying little "spinny-ball" thing pops up, and everything just freezes? (Clearly you recognize my technological prowess.) Man, nothing annoys me more than that darn "spinny ball" and all of the other unexplainable technical glitches that come with computers and phones! I have zero patience for such things. *Everything* is a technical glitch to me because I do not know how to fix, troubleshoot, or solve any problem or even a non-problem related to technology, which makes matters worse! I'm helpless! Utterly helpless!

Which brings me back to my story. I'll admit we were feeling a little helpless. As I mentioned, things were great. And then they were... weird. (Turns out "weird" is my most favorite adjective — just ask my husband.) I won't bore you with the details, but a convergence of factors out of our control had brought our rushing "river of life" (cash flow) to a tiny trickle. The money had already been earned; it just hadn't shown up in the mail. An overdue contract negotiation kept being delayed. Royalty checks were months overdue. Money lent out wasn't being paid back as previously agreed upon. And all these things, all at once. That's what I mean by "weird."

My first thoughts sounded something like this, *Okay, no problem, we've been here a few times. We got this. We're good.* Except weeks turned into months, and it wasn't coming in. A little money would trickle in a bit at a time. But we knew there was *more* than a trickle out there... somewhere! "Hellooo? Lord? You see what's happening here, right? Aren't You going to do something?"

I'll confess there were some moments of confusion and frustration. And maybe a couple of little moments of fear and anxiety. Because that super annoying "spinny ball" thing had descended on our life, and more specifically our bank accounts, and everything was frozen. Questions? Oh sure, we had some of those.

But what we also had was a solid conviction that no matter what, our faith would not be frozen as well. Our trust in our Jehovah-Jireh, the God who provides, would not be shut down by some annoying little spinny ball that appeared on the scene out of nowhere.

We were determined to raise our hallelujah and keep raising it. Declaring the Word of the Lord over our life and our situation. And guess what... even in all those uncomfortable, unfun, loooong weeks of waiting for the financial plumbing to get fixed, God *always* provided just enough to get through the day or the week or to cover whichever automatic withdrawal was happening the next twenty-four hours.

Sometimes it's a banquet table; sometimes it's just manna for today. But it's always and forever the goodness and the faithfulness of God that brings us through. And He is... bringing us through. Even while writing this chapter, we still haven't seen all the money we know is coming through yet. And yes, this is taking longer than we'd prefer, but you know what? It will all work together for our good because we love Him and are called according to His purpose. But the even greater truth is that it will all work together for our good because *He loves us*. He really, really loves us. The King of kings is our good, good Father. And we have zip, zero, and zilch to worry about.

My awareness of my utter dependence on God is what really matters here. My trust in Him for everything and *through* everything is the gold. My husband and I often remind each other that our provision doesn't come from man. Our faith is not in those checks coming in or in the people who owe us money. Our provision comes from *Him* and Him alone. Our *faith* is in *Him* and Him alone.

To be honest, I'm personally very encouraged by the growth I can see and feel in myself during these few difficult months. I draw from past experiences, remembering all the many times God has provided in practical and miraculous ways throughout our lives. "Remembering" is a big deal to God. He instructed his people in the Old Testament all the time to *remember*.

I also draw from my ever-increasing understanding of God's nature and goodness, my knowledge of the kingdom and how it operates. Getting in His presence, poring over His Word, valuing the gift of relationship with Him. It's in this journey with Him that I have been given ample opportunity to see the increase of my faith along the way. So I acknowledge the things that *only* God could have developed in me. I see the work of His hand in my life and give Him the glory for all He has done. I honor Him when I seek to remember and celebrate His work in the world, in others, and in myself.

One thing I've learned about our "ever-increasing faith" is this… it's always for the next step or the next assignment or the next challenge. I will need to draw upon that faith for even bigger faith. He's never done with us. He's always calling us up to higher places in Him. And it is by His grace, lavishly poured over us, that we are enabled to go the distance with Him.

I have also learned this profound lesson. I cannot afford to withhold any hallelujah in any moment or season or circumstance. For it is precisely the hallelujah that carries me through to victory. It's the hallelujah that gives me eyes to see and ears to hear despite all the noise and the fog. It's the hallelujah that roars back at the fake lion who thinks he can get me to doubt the Word of God and succumb to unbelief.

It is *that* hallelujah, the one that is costly and hard, the sacrifice of praise, that strikes the deadliest blow to the enemy and becomes the antidote to everything in my life that tries to "set itself up against the knowledge of God." It is my hallelujah that helps me take those thoughts captive and make them obedient to Christ (2 Corinthians 10:5).

My hallelujah is one of my most valuable and powerful kingdom privileges and assets. And the more of it I use, the more I seem to have.

Any challenge, trial, or circumstance of life that tries to pull my focus away from the goodness of God and tempt me into unbelief needs a hallelujah sung loud in the middle of the storm. That is when I am living in my identity as a beloved daughter of the King. And that is what it means to be victorious!

Whether my feet are roaming the valley or planted on the highest mountain, my God will be praised. Praise is my weapon against the schemes of the enemy. When I raise my hallelujah, the weapon that was formed against me won't prosper (Isaiah 54:17)!

CHAPTER 6:
Don't Pick It Up

It can sometimes be easier to forgive our enemies
than our friends. It can be hardest of all to forgive
someone we love.

— Fred Rogers

Right now… not going to lie — I'm kind of irritated. And I
think I'm kind of angry. And I may be just a bit offended.
I really, *really* do not like feeling these things. I don't mean to
brag, but I've always been an expert at avoiding these kinds of
feelings… you know, the icky ones. The ones that can quickly
become poisonous. But that whole "avoiding" thing… turns
out it's not noble; it's dysfunctional.

Here's what I believe (at least cognitively, still working on
experientially). It is good and healthy to acknowledge my icky,
potentially toxic feelings and emotions. I say "potentially" toxic
because feelings and emotions, in and of themselves, are just
that. Feelings. And emotions. They're initially neither bad nor
good. Except maybe hate. Yeah, that's usually a bad one unless
we know who our true enemy really is (we'll discuss this in a
later chapter).

Anyway, these pesky, icky feelings tend to just strike. And
they can strike at any time. We are not held responsible for
having them. But we *are* held accountable for what we do with

them. To not stuff them or deny them is paramount to our health. Acquiring some self-control so that they don't completely take over and dominate the environment or others is equally paramount to our health. We can feel them and honestly acknowledge they exist. And then, it's good and healthy to let them go. Let them pass through and not take root.

I remember the old cheesy saying, "Let go and let God." *Let God* <u>*what?*</u> I used to think to myself. It was a common hashtag before there were hashtags. But I thought it sounded kind of... well, dumb. I now think what someone was probably trying to say was, "Let go of the things you need to let go of and give them over to God. He will know what to do with them." See, now that makes more sense; it just doesn't make a very good hashtag.

So how do we let things pass through and not take root? A great way to do this is to confess them to God. Because maybe they've become sin or maybe not... yet. Either way, talking it over with Jesus and humbly asking Him to reveal my shortcomings, weaknesses, and failures in the very situation that has got me feeling irritated, angry, and offended is the *best* thing I know to do. But gosh golly, it is *hard*. For me, all of it is hard. I would rather not feel icky emotions because it feels like an assault against my peace. And I really value my peace (another topic we will later discuss).

I have a big confession to make. I like watching the Real Housewives franchise (don't judge). The Real Housewives of... Beverly Hills or Utah or Potomac or New Jersey — it really doesn't matter which one. While each location holds its own flavor and the cultures are unique, there is a recurring theme running through each and every one. Dysfunction! A lot of it. Now just hear me out if you would. I have shallow reasons and deep reasons for watching these shows.

The shallow reasons are that I enjoy observing and comparing the different cultures and environments between the different cities and parts of the country. How the women dress, decorate their homes, entertain and throw parties, where they vacation, how they do holidays, even how they view and relate to their husbands. It's really interesting to me. Kind of like going to the zoo and observing all the different animals. Some are rather endearing, and some are a bit scary. But it's all interesting.

I know some of you are so happy right now that I admitted to liking this entirely frivolous, meaningless show. And then there are some of you that are scratching your head and contemplating whether you will even finish reading this book. So let me finish explaining before you decide.

The deeper reason I like to watch these shows is that I'm often amazed at how so many women become embroiled in constant drama. And it's never their fault, of course. It's always someone else's. The amount of counterfeit confidence and anxiety I see all over these women provokes compassion in me.

I watch perplexed but not surprised. I often imagine myself having a conversation with these women and wonder what I would say to them if I were there in those pain-induced, anxiety-producing, dramatic blowups. How would I respond? How could I use my words and my presence to diffuse the chaos and identify with their core pain? Basically, what could I say or be to them, individually, that would open their heart, even if for a minute, to get a glimpse of God's love? I feel the compassion of God for people on TV. I've been that way for a long time. And to be clear, I don't want to actually *be* on one of those shows, just in case you were wondering. It's absolutely not on my bucket list.

Here's the other thing. I don't aspire to *be* like them; I just sometimes want to be the one to show them the love of the Father. I do not think I'm better than them either. I just know I have found the *better way*, and I want them to find it too. That's Jesus. He's the Way.

So why tell you all this? That's a good question, and here's the answer. It's because although I watch drama on TV, I rarely live it in real life. My friends are solid, grounded, lovely, drama-free ladies, and I like it that way. But once in a while, there will be people in our lives who remind us that life is never drama-free, no matter how hard we try. Drama happens. I wish it didn't.

But here I am, faced with a particularly layered and complex issue. My frame of reference for what *not* to do is to react like a "Real Housewife." Of this I am certain! In this relationship I have steered clear of potential conflict for a very long time. But I am learning there are times when it is appropriate to address things you'd really rather not. And unfortunately for me, that time has come.

Listen, no one likes to be the recipient of little jabs and digs. No one likes to be criticized or scolded. Especially behind their back. No one likes to be wrongly blamed or misunderstood. But you know what can take any mom from zero to a hundred in sixty seconds? When your *child* is criticized, scolded, wrongly blamed, and misunderstood. Just ask the "Housewives." The general understanding, unpardonable sin on this show, according to them, is, "Kids are off limits!" On this, we agree.

As I move ahead and face this relational issue, I am acutely aware of the land mines scattered all around, just under the surface. I must walk very slowly and very carefully. I have no desire to set one off by my own misstep or be the victim of someone else's misstep. The takeaway for me right now is that I am only responsible for my own steps, not for someone else's. I am accountable for each step I choose to take.

This leads me to this vitally important truth. I can only do this right and do this well with Jesus. I belong to a superior kingdom, but that in no way means I am superior. It means I have every resource available to me to respond according to my new nature, not my old one. In order to reflect the beauty of my royal identity, I must go straight to Him, lay it all out, and let Him speak honestly to my heart. He always speaks honestly, but I'm not always willing to listen. I have to be willing to really listen.

James 1:19 (NLT) comes to mind: "Be quick to listen, slow to speak, and slow to get angry."

And for me, right now today, that means *quick to listen to the Holy Spirit.* The Father gave us the Spirit to be our helper. And as a daughter, I've got to listen to everything the Father is speaking through His Spirit. Whether that is conviction, wisdom, redirection, confirmation, *whatever* He is saying, I *need* to hear it. And then I need to respond, and I need to obey. I need to humble myself, confess my wrongdoing, and be honest with God about my thoughts and feelings. He knows them anyway.

I need to humble myself and ask for His help because I have a 0 percent chance of doing this well without him.

James 1:20 (NLT) goes on to finish the sentence like this, "Because human anger does not produce the righteousness that God desires." I'm not entitled to hang on to my anger. I'm not equipped for that. Only God can be trusted with anger and other things like judgment. That is why He says, "Leave that stuff to Me" (my paraphrase).

Whatever God has called us to do He will equip us for. But it isn't always automatic. And that co-laboring requires humility and submission. *He* makes the way, but *I* have to submit to it. I have to intentionally choose it. Over and over again.

These are the nuts and bolts of our relationship with God. It's a *real* relationship. And like any flourishing relationship, it has to include lots of communication. He loves to hear from me. He will always listen to anything and everything I have to say. But I get a whole lot further in life when I spend more time *listening to Him*. What *He* has to say is far more valuable than anything I have to say. Yet, He still lets me speak. I know that I am seen, heard, and known by my Father. But… is He seen and heard and known by me? That's the million-dollar question.

It's rather easy for us to become overly concerned with having our own voices heard in any context or relationship, and that includes our relationship with God. Everyone loves a good listener. But less than everyone puts in the work it takes to *be* a good listener. Just one episode of *The Real Housewives* makes this point crystal clear!

One of the most important aspects of our relationship with Jesus is that we become good listeners. We can freely express everything that's in our hearts to God. The good and the not-so-good. But not at the expense of us not hearing His voice.

The pathway to perceiving the voice of God is paved with humility. At this moment I can't think of one aspect of my life as a follower of Jesus that doesn't require humility, especially as it pertains to anger and offense. We have numerous opportunities, maybe even daily, to pick up offense and anger and hold tightly (again... cue the Real Housewives). It's also true we have the same amount of opportunities to lay it down or not to even pick it up to begin with. You might be thinking, *Well, that sounds a little bit... impossible.* But it's not. We can look at the very thing that strikes at us and say to ourselves, "Don't pick it up."

Proverbs 13:10 says that where there is strife, there is pride.

There is no shortage of strife and pride. It's all around us. What there seems to always be a shortage of is humility. Probably because humility is hard.

I heard many years ago that the best way to walk in forgiveness is to pray for the person you are choosing to forgive. Now at first, that may not sound too difficult if the prayer you're imagining sounds something like this: "Lord, I forgive 'so-and-so' for how majorly stupid and rude they are! I can't believe they did what they did and said all those nasty things. They're just plain awful, and I know how upset *You* must be

The pathway to perceiving the voice of God is paved with humility.

by their horrible offense!" So this is not exactly the kind of prayer I am talking about!

Instead, it's *a prayer of blessing* over their life. When I ask God to pour out His blessing and favor on someone who has hurt me or sinned against me, it, without a doubt, adjusts the posture of my heart toward forgiveness. It requires humility and grace on my part. You cannot hold hate or deep-seated anger in your heart when you are praying for someone's life to be blessed and for them to know the kindness of God.

I've tried it. It works! Praying that kind of prayer for the very one you are choosing to forgive works wonders in your own spirit. There is a release you feel as you pray those words and instantly realize you have loosened your grip on the pain they have caused. And it turns out that pain is usually a good thing to let slip through your fingers. Forgiveness heals us.

So this morning, I found myself keenly aware of my need for humility and my need to forgive. In this current situation, I may not be the source of the strife, but strife is present. Strife was ushered in. And I want to usher it out by the power of the Holy Spirit living in me. Where circumstances and people are involved, I may not have control, but I do have influence. How I proceed matters. How I respond (versus react) and choose forgiveness makes a difference. And it all requires humility. So, in these moments with Jesus, as I seek to eliminate strife, as far as it is up to me, I choose humility, and I choose to forgive.

In case you were wondering what humility sounds like, it's this: "Surely you desire integrity in my *inner* self, and you teach me wisdom deep within. Purify me… and I will be clean" (Psalm 51:6–7, CSB).

"Okay, Lord, I'm ready. Say the hard stuff. Tell me what I don't want to hear. I'll listen. Then I'll respond and repent what I need to repent. I'll do what You're asking me to do. And say what You're asking me to say the way You're asking me to say it. And (maybe even more importantly) I'll stay silent when You tell me to. And above all else, I will forgive because I have been forgiven much and forgiveness sets me free."

This morning before opening my Bible, I prayed this prayer of David from Psalm 51:10 (AKJV). "Create in me a clean heart, O God; and renew *a right spirit* within me." And wouldn't you know, when I did open my Bible, that little silky ribbon bookmark opened right up to Psalm 51. God's funny that way. He's always speaking. Am I always listening?

"Jesus, today...

I will acknowledge my icky feelings and admit they're there. I won't make them an idol or allow them to remain.

I will see them for what they are: potentially toxic.

I will loosen my grip and release my anger, especially my 'righteous' anger (if there really is such a thing), the kind that feels completely justifiable and reasonable.

I will let go of bitterness because that will eat me alive.

I will lay down my offense because You never said I could pick it up in the first place.

I will put all these feelings into Your hands and know that when I do, You will give me the better thing. Love."

Love is the power source for God's kingdom. So love is where my greatest source of power can be found. Love that is patient and kind, gentle and good.

Love that is self-controlled, slow to anger, slow to speak.

Love that is gracious and forgiving. Gracious and forgiving to people who haven't even asked for it and probably never will.

> *"I will do this because You have said that is what I must do. And how dare I not when I have been forgiven so much by You. You have forgiven me of everything, all of it! Even the stuff I'm still too blind to see.*
>
> *And I can't do any of this on my own. I can only do this with You and because of You."*

Anger is extraordinarily easy. It's our default setting. Love is very difficult. Love is the miracle.

When it comes to anger and offense, I won't pick it up. Because they're like stones in the hand: heavy, hard, and potentially harmful. My hands will be free to carry the things you have told me to carry.

Forgiveness, grace, mercy, compassion, humility. When I pick them up and carry them with me into every situation and relationship, I'm sowing good seeds and will reap a harvest of beauty. The beauty of the Holy Spirit's presence and fruit in my life. James 3:18 (NIV) says, "Peacemakers who sow in peace reap a harvest of righteousness."

I think Brant Hansen says it well in his book *Unoffendable*.

> "Grace isn't for the deserving. Forgiving means surrendering your claim to resentment and letting go of anger."

Anger is extraordinarily easy. It's our default setting. Love is very difficult. Love is the miracle.

CHAPTER 7:

Don't Be Nice.
Be Kind

God is so good, that He works *everything* for our
good, even when we don't think it's good.

— Robert Morris

I'm a Heritage Singer. "What, pray tell, is a 'Heritage
Singer'?" you ask. Well, back in 1971 a wonderful man by
the name of Max Mace started a gospel singing group out of
the Northwest. They called themselves the Heritage Singers.
Now, I didn't join the group in 1971 because I was only three
years old and had never heard of them before. But in 1993 I
met a guy who had been singing with them for five years. We
fell in love, and I started singing with them too. I just kind of
fell into it. Goodness knows I would *never* have had the gump-
tion to audition. I didn't do scary things like that. But at the
time, in 1993, they were in desperate need to fill a slot, and I
was the only extra singer hanging around due to that guy I was
in love with. Luckily for them, I wasn't horrible, and lucky for
me, they thought I was a good fit.

I loved it. From the very first moment, I loved it. I quickly
grew to love the people even more. It didn't take long for them

to become family. Same with the guy I was in love with. I married him. Anyway, none of these details are really pertinent to my story, but I wanted to share them anyway. So you're welcome.

I'm coming up on my thirtieth year of singing with "my family." We're always recording new music, but there are many songs that have stuck like glue over the many years. We sing them a lot. One such song happens to have a verse of which I have sung the solo for sixteen years. Now this particular detail is *very* pertinent to the story.

Last weekend we had a big concert in Sacramento. The church was packed. I had been struggling with my voice for several months, mainly due to allergies, acid reflux, and Covid. One thing after another had been affecting my ability to sing like I was used to singing. What I am used to, as it pertains to singing, is not being an amazing vocalist with amazing skill! I am a decent vocalist with limited skill. So the few things I do well in regards to singing feel quite necessary because they're all I got! The frustration I had been feeling for a while was turning into anxiety I'm afraid. And anxiety is not usually a part of my everyday life. I know some people struggle greatly with it. I am grateful that has typically not been my experience… I'm pretty chill. I struggle with laziness and lack of motivation. And eating too much at night.

Things like that. But here I was, faced with some good old-fashioned low-grade anxiety over a short, little, fairly easy solo that I know backward and forward. Remember, sixteen years.

So I decided I was going to tackle this anxiety head-on! I knew what the enemy was up to. He was trying to exploit my weaknesses and intimidate me. I wasn't going to have it. I prayed and repented (of criticizing the voice God gave me). I declared scripture and bound up the enemy in Jesus' name! My vocal cords were going to be fine. I knew it.

So there I was, center stage, poised and ready to sing my solo with vocal cords that had been touched by the Holy Spirit. I opened my mouth, and what came out was actually quite nice. *Oh wow, this spiritual warfare stuff works!* I thought to myself. And then it happened. My cords may have been fine, but my brain was a different matter. I forgot the words. How could I forget the words? I've been singing this song in every concert for sixteen years straight! Are you kidding me right now?

I somewhat gracefully mumbled unintelligible lyrics until I felt so ridiculous, I heard myself say out loud in the mic, "Sorry," with a roll of my eyes. Not the best choice. I might have been able to fake everyone out, but now the cat was out of the bag. I had no clue what I was saying. My dear friends behind me all started throwing out lyrics to help me get back on track. But when I forget a few words, the whole "kit and caboodle" goes out the window. I go blank, and it's over.

I stumbled along in agony, realizing I was so focused on going to battle over my vocal cords, I forgot to include in my prayer "remembering the words." Note to self: when binding up the enemy, don't leave anything out.

When the song finally came to an end, I stepped back and thought, *Well, that just happened.* And then I heard a voice saying, *"Just because you forgot your words doesn't mean I can't still work through the song."* And then I heard, *"You're really not that important."* Now hear me on this. It was not God insulting me; it was God taking the pressure off me. And it was a relief. I was so grateful to hear those words, and it made me chuckle. I've always been pretty good at being able to laugh at myself. It's just easier that way.

God is so gracious, and He is so kind. The Scriptures say He never leaves us nor forsakes us (Deuteronomy 31:8). He's our ever-present help in times of trouble (Psalm 46:1). But that doesn't mean things always go as planned or work out the way we want them to. It means we're not alone and He is a God who redeems. He redeems in huge ways and small ways alike. I know He redeemed my clumsy solo that night. He redeemed every mistake made in that concert. He doesn't need our perfection in order to do His work. We're really not that "important." How is it that we can be so insignificant yet so incredibly valuable to God? It's part of the mystery of His love.

Romans 8:28 (CSB) says that "all things work together for the good of those who love God and are called according to His purpose."

What this does *not* say is that all things are good. That all the things we encounter in this life are directly *from* the hand of God. The enemy has his slimy fingerprints on so much. It doesn't take a genius to look around and see all the *un*-good in this world. All the things never originally intended by God to be a part of the human experience.

So what happened? To put it bluntly, *we* happened. Since the very first human (Adam), we have been given a choice: a choice to partner *with* God and believe *His* words or to partner with the deceiver and believe his words. And both those choices have undeniable consequences for good and for bad.

But God. God was a million steps ahead of us, and *He* had a plan to make it all right. He *has* a plan to return the human experience to all it was perfectly designed and intended to be. The garden of Eden was meant to be a place where everything and everyone worked *with* God in perfect harmony and holy union.

I don't know if you realize this, but God's plan of salvation was *already set in motion* long before Adam and Eve believed the serpent's lie and rebelled against God. We read in 1 Peter 1 that God paid a ransom to save us, and it wasn't paid with gold or silver. It was paid with "the precious blood of Christ, the sinless, spotless lamb of God" (v. 19, NLT). Verse 20 (NLT) goes on to say that God chose Him (His Son) as our ransom "long before the world began."

Do you realize the profundity of what that means? The plan of salvation was not a last-minute "emergency plan." It was *always* the plan. The original design for our destiny included neither sin nor the loss of that perfect existence within the garden. It included the *possibility* of sin because God is love and love allows choice. In His sovereignty, He gave us the free will to choose whom we would believe, whom we would worship, and whom we would obey and serve.

The plan of salvation was always the plan because God knows all and sees all. He lives outside of time and space. He knew sin would enter the world, and He knew we would need a Savior.

Ephesians 1:4–5 (CSB) says that "He chose us in Him, *before* the foundation of the world, to be holy and blameless in love before Him. He predestined us to be adopted as sons [and daughters]." He worked it all out ahead of time because His heart of love was *always for* us. He didn't have to wait and see and then decide if He wanted to save us from the consequence of sin. No. It was never a question.

It's easy for our puny human minds to assume that God only comes up with solutions once a problem is presented. As if He's merely a "quick-thinking troubleshooter." No way. God Himself *is* the solution. So the solution to every problem there could ever be is always at hand. Just like His kingdom is always at hand.

The exciting news is that one day there will be an end to *every problem* and the final solution will be executed when Jesus returns. Until then, the beauty and the majesty of His sovereignty can be worked out in our lives in such a way that even the most painful things that bring sorrow, the most ugly or difficult of circumstances, can and will be reworked, repurposed, reformed, and redeemed for our good and more importantly for His glory. For those who love Him (trust Him, believe Him) and have said yes to the call of His Spirit, the invitation of salvation. Those who are living in their God-designed purpose.

How… ? Well, that's one of the brilliant mysteries of God. Why… ? Because He's that good and loves us that much.

What the enemy means for harm and for evil, the sovereign power of God can transform for our good and for the good of others. And even more importantly, for His glory. That is simply amazing. When I ponder Romans 8:28 and think about God working *all* things together for our good and His glory, I'm intrigued. "Intrigued" is probably not the word you thought I was going to use. Of course, I am grateful for His ability to do this in our lives, but I'm also intrigued. You see, God is able to work all things together for our good because of His power and might. But He does it because of His kindness and goodness.

Most of us are familiar with the fruit of the Spirit Paul speaks of in Galatians 5. It's a list of only nine attributes. I don't know — I would have rounded it up to ten, but that's just me. It's intriguing to me that "kindness" made the list. Spiritually speaking, I think kindness is an underrated and overlooked aspect of holiness. Actually, I would add "gentleness" to that sentiment as well.

Kindness is behind the mercy of God! And where would we be without His mercy? Titus 3:4–5 (NIV) says, "But when the kindness and love of God our Savior appeared, he saved us, not because of the righteous things we had done, but because of His mercy."

Remember a few years back when a popular phrase emerged in our culture? "Random acts of kindness." I liked it. It was meant to encourage our society to be nicer and more thoughtful. I'm not sure, however, that the circulation of this popular phrase really had any significant impact on the culture.

"Nice" is often thought of as considerate, thoughtful, or

> *God is able to work all things together for our good because of His power and might. But He does it because of His kindness and goodness.*

polite. And these are all very good things to be. Nice is good, mostly. But it can have a deceptive side. Niceness can be used to disguise things, sort of like an air freshener used to cover up nasty smells. We can spray our "niceness" over our buried feelings of anger and jealousy, but they're still there, lurking in the shadows. Niceness can cover up our feelings of fear and insecurity. It can veil avoidance. Niceness can even be a false front for hate. That's the thing with niceness. You can't always trust it because sometimes it's not what it seems. And if you still need an example, just think of our politicians. Niceness is show.

Kindness is by far superior to niceness. True, biblical kindness is far deeper and holds greater meaning than your basic, "run-of-the-mill" niceness. Basically, being kind and being nice are really not the same thing. Cultural kindness may be likened to niceness and friendliness, but biblical kindness is far richer and holds power for a mighty impact. Whereas niceness is a surface form of politeness, kindness is an authentic act of love.

Kindness is an expression of love that sometimes isn't even deserved. Kindness is mercy. Mercy often gets confused with empathy. And while it very well can work in tandem with empathy, it is not limited by our empathic emotions. Mercy doesn't require me to *feel* empathetic. I may feel empathetic, but my feelings of empathy, present or not, can never determine whether I will extend or display mercy through acts of kindness. Biblical kindness is, therefore, less random and more intentional.

The kindness of mercy stems from a heart of love, a heart of compassion. Do we ever *feel* love and compassion in our merciful acts and attitudes? Sometimes, yes. But not always.

Sometimes extending mercy and choosing kindness is an act of obedience and a reflection of the heart of our Father.

Merciful kindness does not require me to have feelings of empathy or even love and compassion for a particular person, especially the persons I deem grossly undeserving. Merciful kindness requires my love and devotion to Jesus, period. Out of my love for Him, my love for the unlovable will be made possible.

In fact, do you know that the Bible tells us that a lack of kindness actually brings sorrow to the Holy Spirit? In Ephesians 4:30–32 (NLT) it says, "And do not bring sorrow to God's Holy Spirit by the way you live... Get rid of all bitterness, rage, anger, harsh words and slander... Instead *be kind* to each other, tenderhearted, forgiving one another, just as God through Christ has forgiven you."

Biblical kindness isn't random. It's quite intentional. So what do *intentional* "acts of kindness" look like?

Instead of bitterness, it's forgiveness.

Instead of angry outbursts, it's self-control.

Instead of frustration, it's grace.

Instead of harsh words, it's encouragement.

Instead of criticism, it's praise.

Instead of putting people in their place or avoiding conflict, it's speaking the truth in love.

The stunning words of Jesus in Luke 6:35–36 (MSG) should give us pause. "Love your enemies. Help and give without expecting a return... Live out this God-created identity the way our Father lives toward us, generously and graciously, even when we're at our worst. Our Father is kind; you be kind." It really couldn't be clearer! We don't reflect our royal identity as daughters of the King when we try and justify our choices and behavior by using the unkindness of others as a standard. Our standard for behavior is Jesus. Only Jesus.

Sometimes we have pretty good earthly models of kindness. There are a few select people in this world who seem to overflow with it. I knew one in particular. I watched him live in consistent kindness for almost thirty years. His name was Max Mace. The wonderful man of God who started those Heritage Singers way back in 1971. He went to be with Jesus two years ago, but I will never forget his kindness, gentleness, forgiveness, and grace. He knew how to be the hands, feet, and the mouth of Jesus.

The point is this: I can be passionate and still be kind. I can be right and still be kind. I can be mistreated and still be kind. I can be in disagreement and still be kind. It's never easy, but it's possible. I know it's possible because Jesus said *this* is the way we are to live. I know it's possible because I watched a man who loved Jesus live that way until he died.

There is an exemption clause for kindness, though. And it has to do with spiritual warfare. I am never obligated to be kind to the kingdom of darkness and all the "creatures" of darkness. Satan and his armies are never to be recipients of my kindness, my patience, my gentleness, my goodness, or my love. Only people are. People are redeemable; evil is not. God is impeccably just, and evil will one day come to a screeching halt. But when it comes to flesh and blood, humans created in God's image, no matter how much of evil's influence they are under, I must do and speak all truth in love. And I must be a conduit for the loving-kindness of God, which is mercy, not niceness.

The kindness of God is what takes our shortcomings, our failures, and our sin and mercifully forgives. The kindness of God takes the horrible adversities of life and redeems them for a greater purpose. The kindness of God shows us the way to repentance. Why repentance? Because an unrepentant heart cannot be saved, and He is "not willing for anyone to perish, but for all to come to repentance" (2 Peter 3:9, NKJV).

Kindness is redemptive because Jesus is redemptive. It's a powerful thing of beauty, grace, mercy, and love. And it's His love that makes us more like Him.

PS. — This chapter was unknowingly written on November 5, 2022. Max would have turned eighty-five today.

CHAPTER 8:
Trust and Obey

Obedience is an act of faith; disobedience is the result of unbelief.

— Edwin Louis Cole

There's a song I grew up singing in church called "Trust and Obey." The hook line was, "Trust and obey for there's no other way to be happy in Jesus but to trust and obey." While there is truth in this, I'm going to be honest — this phrase bugged me a little. For whatever reason, sometimes my mind translated this into a picture of an adult standing over me with a wagging, pointed finger and brows raised in superiority, warning me that unless I was always good, I would never be happy.

Some of you might relate in some way, and some of you might be offended by my honest confession. I apologize to whoever wrote this song, as I'm sure this wasn't the intended message. And I don't fault "the church" for my faulty perception either. I blame the enemy, who loves to twist the truth around until it's unrecognizable. And I know he sometimes uses believers to do the twisting, whether they know it or not. I'm aware of the spectrum of missteps within the church at large. They range from well-meaning yet distorted teaching and conduct all the way to insidious, malicious intent and conduct. However, my plumb line is not the church. My plumb line is Jesus, not men and women rife with faults.

I also realize the word "obedience," for some, is a puritanical word that just hits the wrong way. "Religiously" speaking it can provoke thoughts of rule-keeping or a mindset of "salvation by works." And in a culture that is obsessed with personal autonomy and unrestrained freedom, the idea of "obedience" can seem downright draconian.

But faith for the believer is the bedrock of obedience. Without faith, it is impossible to please God (Hebrews 11:6). And without faith it is impossible to *obey* God. The two cannot be separated. And as we know, faith is also closely related and often interchangeable with trust. Most of us are not going to believe, follow, or commit ourselves to someone or something we do not trust. So how do these things all work together? What *is biblical* obedience? What role does obedience play in our spiritual lives? How much does it matter within the context of grace and our relationship with a personal God?

These are important questions to ask and answer. So, at the risk of wading in perhaps deeper theological waters than you would prefer, I want to unpack this idea of obedience. So, stick with me here.

Jesus said, "Whoever hears My commands and obeys them, he is the one who loves Me" (John 14:21). Those are strong words. So the next obvious question for me is this... what exactly constitutes the commandments that Jesus is referring to?

It can be overwhelming and confusing to understand which commandments might be included in this statement that Jesus made. We know it can't be every last commandment ever uttered in the Scriptures, especially the Old Testament. Otherwise, we would still be shopping for unspotted lambs to sacrifice and stoning our neighbors when they broke the law.

Before the cross, detailed and rigorous rule-keeping was the way of life for the Israelites, if for no other reason than to show them just how incapable they were of actually keeping those rules perfectly. The law ultimately revealed their desperate need for the coming Messiah. It reveals the same need for us. Our need for the Savior.

What about all the instructions found in the New Testament? There seems to be a variety of ways believers of different denominations and cultures express their obedience. So how do we navigate through all the apparent "options"? See what I mean? Obedience is a tricky subject to tackle.

A simplified answer could be given when we look closer at the wording of John 14:21. Jesus said, "Whoever hears My commands." A few familiar commands spoken by Jesus come to mind.

To the religious leaders, He said, "Love the Lord your God with all your heart and with all your soul and with all your mind" and "love your neighbor as yourself" (Matthew 22:37 and 39, NIV).

His "sermon on the mount" is full of instructional commands like, "Love your enemies and pray for those that persecute you" (Matthew 5:44, NIV) or "Seek first the kingdom of God and His righteousness" (Matthew 6:33, CSB).

To the twelve, before He sent them out, He said, "Proclaim the kingdom of heaven has come near. Heal the sick, raise the dead, cleanse those with leprosy, drive out demons. Freely you received, freely give" (Matthew 10:7–8, CSB).

And then after His resurrection and before His ascension, He told those disciples to "go, therefore, and make disciples of all nations, baptizing them in the name of the Father and of the Son and of the Holy Spirit, and teaching them to obey everything that I have commanded you" (Matthew 28:19–20, NET).

And these are only but a few examples. Just choosing one command Jesus made and focusing on that would keep us busy until He returns!

The overarching point I wish to make is this: Obedience isn't about rules. It's about the heart. It is not a check-off list that earns redemption. It is a heart posture made possible because of redemption.

When our kids were little, I would very often use this phrase, "I need you to cooperate with me." In essence, I was saying, "I need you to obey me," but asking them to cooperate with me instead felt more nurturing and personal. I would also say to them, "If you choose not to cooperate with me, there will be a consequence." Of course, I would take the time to explain, as much as I could or was appropriate, the "why" behind the need for them to cooperate.

When our son was about three years old, he had been given this familiar directive to cooperate one summer night as we

> *Obedience isn't about rules. It's about the heart. It is not a check-off list that earns redemption. It is a heart posture made possible because of redemption.*

enjoyed dinner outside with his grandparents. But Christian wasn't interested at all in "cooperating" with us. Usually, this parenting approach worked well. It allowed our children to feel like they were being given a fair and informed warning that would give them an empowering opportunity to make a good decision.

But this particular night, it wasn't working. I'll never forget watching my husband get up from the table and briskly scoop up Christian into his arms as he headed inside the house. Right when they got to the door, Christian looked over his dad's shoulder, waved to my parents and me, and said with a smile on his face and a lisp on his tongue, "Bye, guyth, I'm goin' on time out now!" It was so hard not to laugh out loud.

I picture God saying to us, "I need you to cooperate with Me." Or better yet, "*You* need to cooperate with Me because it will go so much better for you if you do." It's not a threat made in anger and frustration. It's an attempt to reveal to us how much we are loved, and every boundary He sets is with us in mind. *He* knows what we don't know, and *He* sees what we can't see. His motivation is always love because God is not a narcissist.

Obedience to God is *so* much more than what many assume it is. Some attach the word "obedience" to merely "good" behavior. What comes to mind are things like going to church, reading the Bible, serving in a ministry. Obedience also gets attached to the idea of "bad" behavior. The laundry list of things we *shouldn't* do. The concept of obedience for some gets reduced to a "Christian chore chart." They've come to assume that this is all God is interested in. A distant Father who only really cares if we've been good and done all our chores. This is *so* sad to me.

A good father pursues his children's hearts! He seeks to have a relationship with them. He understands there are some important chores that he has laid out for them to do. But to a good father, the importance or priority of "getting your chores done'" *pales* in comparison to having a close relationship and heart connection with their child. A good father knows relationship is where the fruit grows. Relationship is where the transformation happens. Relationship is where secure attachment is formed.

Obedience in the kingdom of God is holistic, and it's rooted in personal relationship and personal communication. God may be prompting me to do something that He is not prompting someone else to do. Obedience transcends general principles for all, and it relies heavily on personal connection where each individual child of God can hear the Father speaking just to them. Obedience relies on our developing a sensitivity to the Holy Spirit and His voice, His promptings, His leading. It's that moment when you know God is "asking" you to take a step of faith, and you do. Where God is asking you to have a conversation with someone, and you do. Or to give a financial gift or resource, and you do. To make a courageous decision, and you do. To forgive when it's hard, and you do. To put someone or something else before yourself, and you do. To do the hard work of renewing your mind and speaking heaven's language, and you do. It's all these things and more. True obedience won't be able to manifest in our lives from a list of rules alone. It can only be lived out in its fullest measure within the context of intimate and personal relationship. The heart of a child is connected to the heart of their Father. They know His voice, and they know His love.

Jesus' conversation with a Pharisee on the issue of which commandments he needed to keep helps us out quite a bit in answering all those questions I posed about obedience earlier. Let's go back to the first command of Jesus I mentioned earlier. In Matthew 22:35 a "teacher of the law," who was really only trying to test and trap Jesus, asks Him which commandment was the greatest. And here's what Jesus said, "Love the Lord your God with all your heart, with all your soul and with all your mind. This is the first and greatest commandment. The second is like it, Love your neighbor as yourself" (Matthew 22:37, NIV). That was it. Jesus was saying that our "true north," our "center point" for obedience, is love. Love God with a passion and love people too.

Sometimes it's extremely helpful to simplify it just like Jesus did here. But that doesn't necessarily mean obedience is simple or easy. It takes a willingness to humble ourselves and let God examine our hearts and realign us with His truth. Obedience requires surrender.

I'll tell you a secret. There are a few things that God has spoken in His Word that He and I don't necessarily see eye to eye on. A few things where, if I were God, I would have set it up a bit differently. I probably would have allowed certain things that He doesn't or left out other things that He included. You may be a little bothered by my honesty here, but God isn't. He is way more concerned about my willingness to acquiesce to *His* ways and honor Him as God, laying aside my own opinions and desires, to follow Him. And here is something I have come to earnestly believe. If I did actually 100 percent agree with God on everything or, better yet, fully understood all His boundaries and principles and workings, then I would merely be worshipping and serving a God that I have most likely created in my own image. A diluted version of God that I was totally comfortable with and fully able to comprehend. If you are 100 percent totally comfortable and can fully comprehend *all* of God's directives and principles and ways, then maybe it would be beneficial to examine which parts of Him you may have created in your own image.

I would like to suggest that deferring to the authority and the lordship of God the Father will, at times, be difficult and include acquiescing to principles and perspectives that I don't always like, enjoy, or understand. That is the unavoidable nature of servanthood and sonship. The reality and, ultimately, the beauty of submission within my relationship to God.

In my years of exposure to the various cultures within the body of Christ, I have observed two general schools of thought regarding obedience. The first is viewing our obedience as a means to receive love, acceptance, and forgiveness from God. The other is an underemphasis on the relevance and role of obedience in the life of a believer.

Let me explain. It's as if some people hold proudly in their hands a certificate of completion, which verifies and proves all their good works and acts of righteousness, for the purpose of receiving that stamp of approval that they have made it into the kingdom of God. They've earned their eligibility.

Others hold a certificate of exemption, excusing themselves from the constraints of obedience, because in their minds, once you've been born again and are in the kingdom, then you can pretty much do whatever you want. This is what I like to call the "exploitation of grace." Both understandings of obedience, however, are deeply flawed and will lead to bondage.

Obedience is not what saves us; rather, it is a fruit of being saved. Genuine obedience is what flows out of our lives because of our intimate, personal relationship with Jesus Christ. A love relationship between a perfect Father and His beloved child.

When I have truly encountered the extreme love of God for me and have truly understood the beauty of His grace and gift, then my love for Him cannot help but be expressed through the natural outflow of obedience. I surrender with ease to His ways, without fear or doubt, because I know He is absolute perfection and holy and wholly good. I have truly tasted the sweetness of freedom, true freedom, which is freedom *from* the grip of sin, and I find that I am compelled to follow the One who set me free.

To understand this is to understand what is written in 1 John 4:19.

We love Him because He first loved us! Everything about God is *love*. Everything. To hold tightly to this truth allows me to relinquish my doubt and even my "disagreement" and fully *trust and obey*.

You see, trusting and obeying our Father of love and goodness is designed to be a joy, not a drudgery. As daughters of the King, we are loved beyond measure and cherished beyond comprehension. Living in the light of that love is pure joy. Trust and obedience are the fruit of living in that love.

Did you realize that as daughters of the King, we will one day be rewarded for our "good works," our obedience to Jesus? Many don't have a clear understanding of that reality. I know my understanding wasn't totally clear until I really dug into the Scriptures for myself. Here's my understanding now. The Scriptures do indeed indicate that Christ will determine the rewards that He will give us for our love-motivated obedience and uncontaminated acts of service. Maybe you didn't realize that. While our sins have been buried with Christ and nailed to the cross, we must not assume that our actions, priorities, and values are of no consequence. *Our obedience matters!* Never as a means to earn salvation, but obedience still matters.

Perhaps we have falsely assumed that *because* God's forgiveness has "removed our sins as far from us as the east is from the west" (Psalm 103:12, NLT) and He "remembers them no more" (Hebrews 8:12), there is no need to worry too much about things like "obedience." I find that many people seem to have adopted either the belief that everyone will have to appear before some ominous great and mighty throne of judgment on judgment day or the belief that we believers will have a fast pass and skip right over the throne line. Neither scenario is accurate.

Some of you are getting very nervous — I can tell. And this is probably the point at which I inadvertently adopted a false understanding of a far-off, end-of-times, looming judgment. There was an unsettling version of events that I unknowingly had misunderstood, and all it did was cause a sense of dread. These are subjects often avoided by teachers and pastors. Then again, there are plenty of teachers and pastors who seem to love using these topics to motivate their subjects with fear and guilt. This is worse.

The good news is this. We do *not* have to live with a sense of dread over coming events regarding the day we stand before our King, who sits on the throne. For those who are born again, we have nothing to fear. Let me say that again. Those who have been born again into the family of God have nothing to fear!

So take a deep breath and relax. And don't let the word "judgment" scare you. Why? Because our Father is a just judge. He's a justice warrior against evil. In Him and with Him we are safe and secure. The just Judge who sits on the throne is magnificently good.

And... our Father is a rewarder of those who earnestly seek Him (Hebrews 11:6).

There is a day when God the Father, the just Judge, will be on His throne called the "judgment seat of Christ," and *He will reward us* for our love-motivated obedience and uncontaminated good works. I use these qualifiers for a purpose.

Not all "good works" or "acts of service" are the same. As humans, we don't always do good things for the right reasons. Some works are just for show. Some works have ulterior motives. Some "good works" are complete garbage underneath the surface. We know this to be true. Ultimately, God is the only One who can see deep within the heart of humans and know what is pure and what is not.

Another important factor of understanding rewards in the kingdom is recognizing that there will be many missed opportunities for "good works" that *we* let slip by. Those will result *not* in punishment but in a *loss* of reward. God will justly "judge" (evaluate and weigh) all these things and determine how each of us individually will be rewarded. "For we must all appear before the judgment seat of Christ so that each of us may receive what is due us for the things done while in the body, whether good or bad" (2 Corinthians 5:10, NIV).

We do need to acknowledge, however, that there is a frightening side to God's judgment, but we don't need to be frightened by it. Let me explain…

What we may have considered to be frightening regarding God's end-time judgment is, in actuality, His just judgment against evil. The forces of evil work through the kingdom of darkness. And when I hold that perspective, I find myself far more relieved and even excited that all the forces of evil will be judged, sentenced, and come to an end. At some point the vast kingdom of darkness will be banished into the abyss never to be seen again!

Sin will absolutely be judged. God would not *be* a just God if He did not judge sin and evil. The question then is, "Whose sin will be judged?" The short answer is anyone whose sin has not been covered by the blood of the lamb. It's the rejection of God's love and gift of salvation that leaves one's sin uncovered.

Yet, the stumbling block for so many is their own faulty assumption of the nature of God, which is often based on an incomplete idea of a distant, angry, sadistic God judging decent people with a harsh, eternal punishment because they didn't believe in Him. We are not helpless victims of an angry god. We are His creation in need of a Savior. So a Savior He became.

> *We are not helpless victims of an angry god. We are His creation in need of a Savior. So a Savior He became.*

Romans 3:23 (NIV) says that "*all* have sinned" (even decent people) and have "fall short of the glory of God." God is the only One without sin. He's the only One perfectly perfect. "God is light and there is absolutely no darkness in Him" (1 John 1:5, CSB). His kingdom is perfect; His ways are perfect. His love is perfect. No one could ever come close to that kind of perfection. No one has what it takes to live in the holy and awesome presence of God without being justified to do so. God knew this, and so He provided us the *opportunity* to be justified. He doesn't force this on anyone. To be justified is to be made "acceptable" and is what is required for us to live eternally with Him. His love did that. His love made a way.

The righteousness *of* God is given to us *by* God, like a beautiful cloak that He takes from Himself and lovingly wraps around us for our benefit. Romans 3:22 says that righteousness is given through faith in Jesus Christ to all who believe. He won't force the "cloak of righteousness" on us, however. It's offered to all, and all who receive it will live. Everything about God is love. Second Corinthians 5:21 (MEV) says, "God made Him who had no sin [his son] to be sin for us, so that in Him we might become the righteousness of God." That, my friend, is *love*.

To deny the relevance or even the existence of what the Bible calls "sin" is problematic. First John 1:8 says (CSB), "If we say, we have no sin we are deceiving ourselves, and the truth is not in us. But if we confess our sin [acknowledge our fallen state and need to be saved], He is faithful and just to forgive us our sins and to cleanse us from all unrighteousness."

The stubbornness and pridefulness of men and women are the only things keeping them from encountering the only love that is able and willing to *save* them from themselves and their own natural, fallen state of sin's decay. To save them from the effects, if you will, of evil forces working endlessly to keep them in the dark and blind to the truth. That is the only thing God hates. *Sin* and *evil*. Because sin and evil are responsible for destroying people's lives. They relentlessly intend to hinder us from surrendering to His love.

You see, at the risk of oversimplification, it's not so much that God will judge *people* as it is God will judge sin. The sin in people that has not been covered by His own righteousness, that has not been washed in the blood of the Lamb, will be judged. And that just judgment of sin absolutely holds consequences for people. People are, in a sense, collateral damage. And that breaks His heart. But justice must be served. And He is unable to break His own law of justice because He has no sin.

To summarize all this heavy stuff, I will say this. Love does not condemn. Sin is the condemner. And God is the One who made a way for all to be saved *from* sin and condemnation because "God is love" (1 John 4:8).

The most famous verse in all of Scripture has to be John 3:16 (NIV): "For God so loved the world that He gave His one and only Son, that whoever believes in Him will not perish but have everlasting life." This one sentence is a beautiful summary of the epic love story of God and His creation. But I wish John 3:17–18 (NIV) was as well known: "For God did not send His Son into the world to condemn the world but to save the world through Him. Whoever believes in Him is not condemned, but whoever does not believe stands condemned *already*, because they have not believed in the name of God's one and only Son." Meaning humankind stands condemned already because of sin. **Sin decays and destroys. Jesus saves and makes new.** It is sin that will be justly judged by God. Those who refuse to see sin for what it really is and fail to recognize their desperate need to be saved won't be.

I really hope this insight of our future rewards given to us by our loving Father extinguishes all fear and lights a fire of passion within your heart to live with intentionality and purpose as you trust and obey.

As I hope you've realized by now, the "judgment seat of Christ" is different. As we stand before this throne, our sins will *not* be drudged up from "the depths of the sea" (Micah 7:19) and brought up for discussion only to be used against us. We will *not* be made to answer for all of our sin that was nailed to the cross. We won't be judged for our sin because Jesus took that judgment that we deserved upon Himself on the cross. And that work is *complete*.

We will *not* stand before this throne in shame. Shame was nailed to the cross as well. We will *not* stand before this throne in competition or comparison. This is a personal encounter with our loving Father in heaven, where our life will be weighed and measured, and every opportunity we took to serve Him, obey Him, and represent Him well is rewarded.

This is why I'm compelled to drive home the point that obedience matters. Our priorities matter. Our choices matter. Not to scare us into compliance but to open our eyes to the love of a good Father who delights in *rewarding* us, His beloved daughters.

Jesus said:

> Do not store up for yourselves treasure on earth,
> where moth and rust destroy and where thieves
> break in and steal. But store up for yourselves
> treasures in heaven, where neither moth nor rust
> destroys, and where thieves don't break in and
> steal. For where your treasure is, there will your
> heart be also.
>
> — Matthew 6:19–21 (CSB)

Every gracious act of God is a *gift* and never an excuse to undervalue the power of trust and obedience, which are the expressions of our faith. Obedience not only requires trust, but it also requires humility, surrender, sensitivity to the Holy Spirit, and wisdom. Obedience at its core is the beautiful outflow of servanthood and gratitude from a heart that has been transformed by love.

CHAPTER 9:
When It's Green, Go

God is looking for people through whom He can
do the impossible. What a pity we plan to do only
things that we can do ourselves.

— A. W. Tozer

"Oh, okay, God, I see... we're living in Babylon." This
was my epiphany while sitting at a red light on Santa
Monica Boulevard. This epiphany was quickly followed by
a picture of Shadrach, Meshach, and Abednego in the fiery
furnace they had been thrown into. It was their punishment
for not worshipping the empire's famed King Nebuchadnezzar
and conforming to the pagan culture in which they were exiles.

Many of you probably know how the story goes. The three
dudes with the funny names were in the fiery furnace completely unharmed and unaffected by the flames surrounding
them. Clearly, this is what we would call a miracle. One of
those crazy, unbelievable, standout miracles of the Old Testament. A popular Sunday school story I saw being played out
on that infamous flannelgraph board of my childhood.

This picture of these three brave, God-fearing men, literally standing in flames, completely protected from any harm,
resulted in my next epiphany. "And Babylon is where we will
see the greater miracles." Because the further you step outside

of your comfort zone and wade into foreign territory, especially hostile enemy territory, the more necessary miracles are. The third epiphany that quickly followed was this, "…and no harm will come to us." Meaning no matter what the enemy throws our way, he will never have the victory over us! Then the light turned green, and I continued on to the grocery store.

Let me bring you up to date. Since writing the previous chapter, we moved. A move we knew was coming at some point in our lives, but we had no idea when it would be. Several years ago, God put a picture in my mind of our family relocating from Irvine, California, which is located in the middle of Orange County. A beautiful, safe, relatively affluent suburban area of Southern California. I saw us relocating up to the Los Angeles area, which is completely different. It's only about fifty miles north, but it may as well be a totally different state. This "relocation picture" wasn't so much a desire as it was a vision of where God would take us, and it was connected to an assignment or a calling that He would give us.

This picture God put in my heart was vivid and detailed. I saw a home filled with people who were gathered inside worshipping, sharing, learning, giving, receiving, laughing, and crying. The presence of God was palpable. Miracles of healing were taking place. Physical, emotional, and spiritual healing. There was such a strong atmosphere of love. God's love being poured out on individuals who had either been following Him for a long time or had just met Him for the first time. There were broken people, lost people, found people, curious people, stumbling people, and sure-footed people all gathered together for basically one purpose. To "taste and see that the Lord is good!" (Psalm 34:7, NIV).

As I shared this vision with my husband, he was in instant agreement. The picture of this future reality resonated deeply in both of our hearts. *How* this would happen and *when* this would happen, we had *no* clue. But *that* it would happen seemed right and true. We had faith for it. We believed it to be from God. We would wait on the Lord and seek His confirmation and His timing. We were not in a hurry by any means, but it seemed rather "reasonable" to us that within a year or maybe two, we could actually be moving. But here's the thing: God rarely does things according to our idea of what's reasonable or what makes sense to us.

It would be over six years later when God would finally give us the "green light" to make a move. It was very sudden. I mean totally out of the blue for us. On May 9th, 2022, moving wasn't even *close* to being on our radar. On May 10th, it was crystal clear. There's too much to this story to unpack now, but within days we had met with our realtor, and a few weeks later, our home was prepared and on the market to sell. Several weeks after that, we were loading up the truck and moving up to Los Angeles.

Did I have doubts at times during those six years? Yes, occasionally I would question the vision. Wondering if what I had seen and felt the Lord saying was really Him or just a fanciful idea on my part. But moving through those moments of doubt and questioning always left me more convinced and increased my faith for what God had shown us.

As always, God's timing was impeccably perfect! Just weeks before our sudden "green light," our son had made plans to move out of the house for the first time and relocate to the San Diego area, where God had so graciously laid out a path for him to follow. A new strong Christian friend and room- mate, a new job, and a new church family were waiting for our son, and God had provided all that for him at just the right time. He was taken care of beforehand so that when our green light came on, this mom's heart could rest assured knowing her son was happily beginning a new chapter of his young adult life. And our relocation wouldn't have an adverse effect on him in any way. I will forever be grateful to God for that gracious display of kindness and love.

Our daughter turned eighteen on May 10th, the very day God gave us our "green light." And I don't believe for one second that this was a coincidence. Our daughter turning eighteen represented a major transition. She was wrapping up high school and launching full time into her career aspirations, which had always included moving up to LA. Now the three of us would do that together. My husband has been working in the entertainment industry since arriving in Southern Cal- ifornia in 1999, and he had been commuting up into the city for over two decades. Now those days would be over. A huge advantage for moving. But in many other ways, the advantages were few.

As I mentioned earlier, the idea of moving out of Orange County and into a major city fraught with soaring crime rates, a rampant homeless population, cramped streets and build- ings, horrible traffic, ridiculous housing prices (considering the location), more oppressive government overreach, and flagrant, undisguised demonic activity was not what I would call a *desire*. It makes *no* sense to leave a much safer, cleaner, lovelier, spacious, and family-friendly environment to go live in the opposite. Unless it's God. Unless it's a dream, a calling, an assignment, or a vision inspired by God Himself and given to us to run with. In that context, it makes all the sense in the world.

I'll be honest — there were times, especially when 2020 hit, that I would be driving around Orange County thinking, *God, are You still sure about this LA thing? 'Cause if You want to change the plan, I'm okay with that! I'm very content and happy in Orange County.* Things in Los Angeles had exponentially worsened with the onset of the pandemic and all the residual damage it brought to Los Angeles, like many cities in the US. But as I would surrender my apprehension and concerns to Him, His peace would once again reassure me it would all play out according to His will, and we would be more than okay as we walked with Him in obedience and child-like trust.

Here's the truly amazing part of this whole story. We love it here! We love living here in Babylon, complete with lion's dens and fiery furnaces! And the only reason why is because of Jesus. When you are partnering with Him and living out the assignment He has called you to, He gives you a grace that is beyond measure for what you are doing or, in our case, where you are living. It doesn't make any sense at all that I don't miss even one little bit where I used to live. I feel warm and fuzzy sentimental thoughts about where we lived. But I do not miss it.

Oh and did I mention the other enormous gift God gave to us in the months leading up to that pivotal "green light" day? You may want to sit down for this one. Sixteen years ago, we stood in our driveway saying our tearful goodbyes to our dearest friends as they set off to move to St. Louis. More than once or twice it was said that they would *never* move back to California, and especially *not* LA! Well, God had other plans, and they have just recently moved back to California. And yes, they are in Los Angeles. About a mile away from us. They have been in full-time ministry their entire married life, and they have been well acquainted with our vision for years now. But it wasn't until the beginning of this year, 2022, that God began to radically shift their own vision for their own family.

Months before our "green light" day, they received a green light of their own and knew that they knew God was leading them to take their beautiful dream home, located in a quaint upscale Chicago suburb, and put it up for sale for the purpose of relocating to Los Angeles. Crazy. Absolutely crazy. This was the sentiment of many around them and to them as well. Yet, they responded to this "unreasonable, illogical" invitation with an enthusiastic *"yes!"* They embarked on the biggest leap of faith they had ever taken and prepared to move across the country with no particular job or home waiting for them on the other side. At one point this spring, I said to my husband, "Could it really be that the Reeds will end up in LA before *we* do? How crazy is that?"

Turns out we ended up moving within a month of each other without any coordinated efforts on our parts. To say that this was one of the most amazing things to transpire in this story is an understatement of enormous proportions. It was the gift to beat all gifts! God bringing our families back together, in close proximity, for a purpose greater than ourselves and calling us into a partnership was beyond what we had imagined. This was a major Ephesians 3:20 event!

"Now to Him who is able to do exceeding abundantly above all that we ask or think, according to the power [of His Holy Spirit] that works in us, to Him be the glory" (Ephesians 3:20–21, NKJV).

And just in case you're wondering, they love LA just like we do! And it makes no sense to them either! They moved into a very nice two-bedroom apartment complex with a cozy balcony (that's a nice way of saying tiny) where the pungent smells of the city would waft up the six-story building and greet them like a warm cup of disgusting coffee. Nothing that twenty toxic-eating, stink-removing plants can't handle, however. They love this place. Go figure.

This has been a theme in our conversations as we have marveled together over the grace God has given all of us for this major transition. The love and compassion *He* has filled our hearts with for this city and its people is something only He could do.

I would like to circle back to the idea of "Babylon" and "enemy territory." First of all, I recognize that every nation, city, community, or village on the planet is in need of the transformative power of Jesus Christ. There are lost people in every corner of the globe. But I think it safe to say that there are territories where the kingdom of darkness weighs significantly heavier. An almost tangible presence of evil looms thicker in certain areas than in others. Places where the enemy's agenda to "kill, steal, and destroy" is heartbreakingly on display in the most obvious of ways.

In ancient history, Babylon was one such city. Satan was the god of that place, and it showed. Today there are many "Babylons" where Satan's influence has had a devastating effect on the society and culture.

However, it is crucial to differentiate between human individuals and forces of evil.

Ephesians 6:12 (CSB) says, "For our struggle is not against flesh and blood, but against the rulers, against authorities, against the cosmic powers of this darkness, against evil, spiritual forces in the heavens."

In Ephesians 2:2 (CSB) Satan is referred to as "the ruler of the power of the air," and it says that he is the "Spirit now working in the disobedient."

He is the one behind *all* the horrible consequences of sin and death. The ones we see every day affecting people's lives in a myriad of ways. The destruction, disaster, and decay that is left in the wake of the evil one, who speaks lies and lures people into all kinds of rebellion against God, is tragic, but it doesn't have to be the end of the story! *Every person, every situation, and every circumstance is redeemable because of Jesus and the power of the cross!*

It's true we have free will to choose whom we will serve and follow. Mankind has always played a part in its own demise. But we must see beyond the physical world into the spiritual world. We must remember that people, in and of themselves, are never really our enemy. Even the very worst people we can think of. The really bad ones. They still, in all their wickedness, are not in the big, spiritual picture, the actual enemy.

This perspective is what allows us to look behind and beyond the horrors of humanity and see redemption is always possible. This perspective moves us closer to seeing others and the world around us like Jesus does, with an *undeserved* and *unreasonable* compassion.

Just for a bit of clarification, I will ask this question. Is it right to take measures to protect ourselves and others from such individuals or groups of individuals who pose a direct threat to the well-being, safety, and health of our families, communities, cities, and nations? *Yes*, of course! There is no denying we have actual physical enemies in our world. Whether they are burglars, murderers, sexual predators, horribly corrupt governments, maniacal dictators, abusive spouses or relatives, just to name a few. "Enemies" come in all shapes, sizes, colors, and costumes. And exercising wisdom and seeking justice is necessary. I may have compassion for the shady characters I observe lurking in the shadows, but I'm still locking my doors at night!

My point here is that our ability to recognize the spiritual forces behind these "enemies" is perhaps the most crucial element of all. Our true enemy is the deceiver, Satan. And it is because of Christ that we have victory over him! Remember in Luke 10:19, when Jesus told His disciples that He had given them the power to "trample over snakes and scorpions"? He wasn't referring to the reptiles and gigantic bugs that they might have found along the hot, dusty roads of Israel.

The disciples had been sent out in twos to go on ahead of Jesus into all the towns and villages that He would be visiting. When they returned, they were filled with joy as they reported to Jesus, "Lord even the demons submit to us in your name!" (Luke 10:17, CSB).

I imagine these grown adults were like little kids returning home from summer camp in such a state of excitement over all that they had experienced. Jesus followed up their recounting of events with His own recounting of events when He told them, "I watched Satan fall from heaven like lightning! Look, I have given you the authority to trample on snakes and scorpions and over all the power of the enemy; nothing at all will harm you" (Luke 10:18–19, CSB).

These two little verses are like two small, priceless gems "hiding" in plain sight. They are bursting with valuable truth. We, too, as followers and disciples (learners) of Jesus, have this same authority! Are we using it? Maybe, like so many others, you have never even realized the full extent of what you have access to as a child of the King in His kingdom.

So when I speak of moving into a hostile, enemy territory, I am not referring to individuals. I am referring to the "ruler of the power of the air" and "the spiritual forces in the heavens" that work tirelessly toward our destruction and demise. I have found that most unbelievers and, sadly, too many professing Christians have no clue what is really going on behind the scenes as it pertains to their own lives and the lives of those around them. Even if they're not blind to the *effects* of darkness, they are still largely blind to the *source* of darkness. Satan and his demonic forces resonate in their imaginations more as a fairy tale than as an actual, consequential reality.

The kingdom of darkness is real, and it is more complex than we often realize, but it is not the strongest force, nor is it the largest force. The kingdom of God is greater by far. And His is a kingdom of love. The love of God can pierce through any darkness, at any time, in any way, in any person. And God uses *us* in the process of piercing the darkness. God doesn't need us in any way, shape, or form to help Him out, but for whatever reason, He has chosen to do so. It's a radical move on His part, but more than that, it is a privilege and a mandate. It's a part of our purpose by His design.

When God gives you "the green light," don't hesitate. Just go. Go into that situation, that assignment, that place, knowing that whatever He calls you to, He will equip you for. Just like the seventy-two who were sent out in pairs to minister to the people in preparation for Jesus. They unequivocally needed the power and the authority given to them in order to do the very thing they had been sent to do. It would have been impossible otherwise. God knows that without Him we don't have what it takes, not by a long shot. But sometimes I wonder if *we* really know that. Not just in theory but in practice.

If you stop and think about it, how often do we rely largely on our *own* skill set, our *own* gifting, our *own* education or experience to serve God? I'm not implying this type of service is of no value, but it doesn't require any trust. It doesn't require anything beyond what we're capable of doing on our own.

Go into that situation,
that assignment, that place,
knowing that whatever He calls you to,
He will equip you for.

In Matthew 14 we find the account of "Jesus feeding the 5000." Another very popular "flannelgraph board" story. I can still see the little fish and the basket of bread suspended up on that felt board next to Peter, James, John, and Jesus. I'm pretty sure the paper cutouts of Peter, James, and John were used in every single flannelgraph story, no matter who the story was actually about, because those three seemed to be up on that flannel-graph board every Sunday morning. By the way, the "Peter, James, and John in a sailboat" story was always a hit. Complete with its own song and hand motions!

But I digress… let me summarize the feeding of the 5000 story. The massive crowd following Jesus around was hungry. It was getting late. The disciples advised Jesus to send them away to the villages to buy food. Not the most brilliant idea. Imagine over 10,000 people (because 5000 only numbered the men) dispersing in an orderly fashion to walk the several miles back to a little village, only to stand in line for food, if that was even a thing back then. And what village could accommodate feeding thousands of people with no advance notice? What were they thinking?

And then, Jesus responds to their brilliant idea with this brilliant idea, "They don't need to go away," He says. "*You* give them something to eat" (v. 16, NIV). Now, any critical thinker would stop at this point in the story and ask, "What in the world was Jesus thinking?" I mean, really, what were these ordinary dudes gonna do? I would have loved to have seen the look on their faces when they looked down at the five loaves and two fish they had in their possession and then looked back up at Jesus. "I'm sorry, Rabi, do what now? This is all we have!"

But Jesus answered, "Bring them here to me" (v. 18. NIV). The five loaves and two fish, that is.

Jesus did not need their involvement. He did not need their ideas. He did not need their two cents or their two fish. He needed them to see their own limited realm of what was possible. He needed them to see that with God *anything* was possible. Jesus could have taken care of the food problem without involving any of them in any way. But He didn't. He invited them to be a part of the solution, even though He knew they were utterly incapable of solving the problem alone. They had next to nothing to contribute except a willingness to *trust* and *believe*. And that was exactly what Jesus was looking for!

Where in your own life do you have next to nothing to offer? What in your life requires way more than your own skill set, gifting, education, or experience? What are those circumstances, aspirations, problems, or dreams that can only be resolved, attained, solved, or realized with the supernatural hand of God intervening because without Him it would be impossible? Are you willing to look beyond this limited, earthly realm and see with eyes of faith all that is possible with God? Are you willing to surrender to what you consider "reasonable" and to trust and believe that the God you serve is famous for doing the "unreasonable" because He is subject to no limitations?

When Jesus said to the disciples, "*You* feed them," I think He was trying to teach them a very valuable lesson. (Duh… ! And now clearly my own brilliance is showing.) What they could in no way do on their own, they could absolutely do with their miracle-working God. They weren't being asked to do it alone, and they weren't being asked to sit this one out and just let God do all the work (the two very common options or mindsets employed by most of us). No, they were invited to partner with Jesus in faith and surrender. And as they did, the loaves and the fish began to miraculously multiply before their very eyes.

What or where is your Babylon? In what or where do you desire to see miracles? To see, feel, and know the mighty hand of God intervening in such a way that only He could receive the glory and the honor because only He could have done that impossible thing!

For now, as I mentioned before, Los Angeles is our Babylon. But Los Angeles is more than that. It is also the "City of Angels." And I believe that wholeheartedly! I know that there is an unmatchable force of angel armies that are active and working in this city. The history of this place is rich with the mighty moves of God. Revelation and revival are a part of its very DNA. There are believers posted all around this city, ready and willing to be the hands and feet of Jesus. Ready to partner with God in bringing about His kingdom here on earth. There is a harvest, and the "Lord of the harvest" is the miracle-working Redeemer of all.

There is a green light for all of us. A call to *go*. Go into our Babylon, in whatever form that may be, and take up the authority given to us by Jesus the King. Whether that's in relationships, in finances, in families, in all matters of health, in workplaces, in homes, in communities, in states, and in nations. When we find ourselves in places of deeper waters, places where the miracle-working hand of God is an absolute necessity, we must not be afraid but rather filled with an expectant hope and a disciple-like excitement, knowing that this is our Babylon, where the greater miracles are, and no harm will come to us.

Just like a snake who is without arms or legs, Satan has been disarmed and defeated. He was defeated at Calvary. He's already lost, but he keeps on fighting by means of lies and deceit. The only power he truly has is when we believe his lies, no matter how big or how small. I heard once, "Believing the lie empowers the liar!"[1] Oh, how true that is.

There will come a day at the end of the age when his ability to even speak one more lie will be done! He will be utterly vanquished for all time. Until then, we must be clear about whose we are and whose authority we are under and have access to. We must live with a full understanding of the victory we have been given the privilege of walking in.

Go into your Babylon with the authority and power of heaven backing you up. Wait and watch with expectant hope for the mighty hand of our miracle-working God to show up and do what only He can do as you walk in faith, surrender in trust, and live in obedience to *His* will and *His* ways, which are always far superior to ours. The green light is your invitation to partner with Him.

---

1   From a sermon by Bill Johnson

CHAPTER 10:
Get Your Hopes Up

Everyone who has been born of God has
conquered the world. This is the victory that has
conquered the world: our faith.

— 1 John 5:4 (CSB)

I love singing songs about heaven. I love singing songs about
the return of Christ! They are filled with so much hope and
remind us that this world and these bodies we live in are *so*
temporary. There *will* be a day when Jesus Christ returns and
establishes the new heavens and the new earth.

Jesus, the Lamb of God, took on the sin of the world so we
could be clothed in the righteousness of God and set free from
sin, the ultimate slave master. The work of the cross and the
power of the empty grave won the victory over sin and death.
And because of love, that victory is ours as well! As new creations in Christ, we are called to *live* from that place of victory
and power in the here and now while living with the promise
of a glorious, heavenly future for all eternity.

That is the gospel. The good news. And the promise of His
return is among one of the very best promises He has made to
us. But I have been challenged by something I heard recently,
which is this: "Many of us have more faith in the return of

Christ than we do in the power of the gospel."[2] Now the power of the gospel is 100 percent responsible for our eternal home in heaven. Most of us realize that. We are grateful beyond words for that. And it *is* a joy to celebrate that.

But, if you take a second and look around, you'll find that there are those whose hope is sorely lacking joy. Their existence on this earth reflects a "joy-deficient mentality" that places *more* focus on a "future rescue mission" from the power of darkness than it does on our *present* foundation of faith, which is the power of the gospel, not just for eternity but for the here and now. It's as if they've forgotten that the power of the gospel not only changes their future destination, but it also changes their present reality as well!

Guess what? It's big enough to do both! And I believe that Jesus is returning for a victorious church, His beautiful bride. Not a pathetic, anxious, fearful, cowering church. What does it say to those around us about the God of the universe who created us in love, returning to a people living virtually powerless lives while hiding under their preverbal rocks? Many Christians are feverishly intent on avoiding the darkness of the world *at the expense* of living in this world as joyful, peace-filled, hope-obsessed, powerful overcomers!

Romans 8:11 tells us that the very same Spirit that raised Jesus from the dead lives in *us!* When we live wide awake to that reality and come into alignment with that power, we won't be a people consumed with the distraction of an escapism mentality. It is our privilege to live *now* in the power of the gospel, which is *far* above every other power. Period. And it is our present joy and hope to know that someday we will "be

---

2   From a sermon by Bill Johnson

like Him because we will see Him as He is" (1 John 3:2, CSB). The power of the gospel affects both the "then" *and* the "now."

I would like for us to revisit some of what I wrote about in chapter 2. The beauty of true hope, joy, peace, and love. Let's start with hope. The world needs *hope*. But in the absence of any kind of understanding of God or relationship with Him, where do they find it? Not a temporary, flimsy sort of hope. But an anchored, unshakeable kind of hope. The world's idea of hope is nothing more than a type of wishful thinking. A desire without any guarantee. It's a "hope" based in self-effort or, even worse, luck.

I heard a pastor once define *hope* like this: "The joyful anticipation of the goodness of God."[3] I love this definition. Because this kind of hope is firmly rooted in the absolute faithfulness of God. And that is what makes it unshakable.

> *Living in hope and with hope will result in a life marked by joy and peace.*

This biblical definition of hope also highlights that real hope includes joy. Taking it one step further, we can say joy-filled hope includes peace. To have hope infused with joy is to have a kind of peace that surpasses all understanding, which the Bible calls the "peace of God" (Philippians 4:46). Living in hope and with hope will result in a life marked by joy and

---

3   From a sermon by Bill Johnson

peace. The beautiful fruit of the Holy Spirit. When we lack joy and peace, we're probably lacking hope.

It is worth mentioning here that biblical joy is different from what we would call happiness. Happiness is awesome. It's not unbiblical, frivolous, or shallow. No, happiness is sweet, fun, and delightful. Let's face it — most of us find happy people uplifting and refreshing to be around. Now I know there are a few of you hardcore "melancholics" who find happy people highly suspect and somewhat annoying. But for the rest of us, they're mostly enjoyable.

Joy is different, though, in that it doesn't rely on favorable circumstances or events, and it isn't connected to a particular personality bent or type. Joy is for everyone. Even you hardcore melancholics. Joy is that God-breathed phenomenon that remains securely fastened in the deepest parts of us. We can be grieving and still have underlying joy. We can be heartbroken and still hold on to joy. We can be sorrowful and still possess the joy of the Lord. Why? Because Joy transcends happiness.

I picture it like this: The solid-like-steel pillars underneath the water that hold up bridges. The waters could be still and quiet, or they could be violently crashing about. Either way, the underwater pillars are unmoved. They remain. This is joy.

Joy is strength. Not our own strength but the strength of the Lord abiding in us as we abide in Him. Nehemiah 8:10 (CSB) says, "The joy of the Lord is your strength." Within the context of this verse, the Hebrew word for joy is *chedvah*, meaning "gladness." The Hebrew meaning of the word "strength" in this verse is "a place of safety," a "refuge," or a "stronghold." When God is our everything, our soul and spirit are assured of having a constant place of refuge and safety, *regardless of our circum-stances*. And that assurance makes us glad, which is joy.

"For you O Lord have made me glad by your work; at the works of your hands I sing for joy!" (Psalm 92:4, ESV).

Joy is medicinal. It heals and soothes. The "oil of gladness" mentioned in Isaiah 61 is given for mourning. In ancient times, oils were used in the practice of medicine. Healing oils were applied to wounds for healing purposes. Joy is like a healing oil applied to the wounds of our hearts. The presence of joy is Jesus with us and in us, which is the assurance of the refuge we will find in the strength of the Lord. It's not pretending to be happy while stuffing or denying our emotions. Rather, it is the strong, nurturing, hope-filled presence of the Holy Spirit in our lives, filling us with the peace of God.

Peace, according to the world, is the absence of something. The absence of war or strife. And for some of us, peace can be the avoiding of something or someone. But the peace of God is different. Simply put, it is not the absence of something but the presence of someone. The same pastor who shared the above definition of hope is the same one who defined peace this way. And I love this definition as well.

There is a particular personality type that places a very large value on peace. They seek it, they crave it, and they start to get very nervous when their own peace is under threat. I'm somewhat of an expert in this area because this personality type happens to be mine.

Peace, or the understanding of peace, can be tricky. One of the more notable strengths of my personality type is the presence of peace. I've been told over and over that my words, my approach, and my presence in a place or a situation bring a sense of peace. Many friends and visitors who have come to our home over the years have made very similar comments about how our home is always so peaceful, like an oasis.

I must admit, when I hear these things, I'm delighted. It's one of the best "words of affirmation" I could hear. And it's not because I'm so proud of myself for doing something amazing or spiritual or for doing something difficult. For me it's not that difficult. It's more "natural," and I happen to value it. I believe the reason I value and release peace to the extent that I do is because it's deeply embedded in my DNA. It's my design. God put it there, and I can't take the credit for it.

The flip side of my natural tendency to value and, therefore, foster peace is not so praise-worthy. It can become somewhat of an idol. Something I crave for my own benefit, comfort, or self-protection.

Something that I will go to great lengths for, such as sub-conscious denial, unhealthy avoidance, disconnection, or toler-ance. Tolerance can be a virtue until it isn't. The truth is this: tolerating the wrong thing doesn't really lead to peace.

Some things in life need to be met "head-on" in a healthy way, even when that means there will be discomfort, disagree-ment, or necessary division. Those are things that can make a peace-loving personality break out into hives. At least inter-nally. We don't like making other people feel uncomfortable, so we break out into hives on the inside. Isn't that thoughtful?

Manipulating my environment to avoid a painful reality that needs attention is not a healthy way to find or make peace. That's pretend peace, and it doesn't really work that well in the long run. Peace*makers* are far more beneficial and valuable than peace*keepers*.

The *making* of peace in our environment, our homes, our family, our relationships... even our problems, our contentions, or any of the storms in our lives, is something that the Holy Spirit does in us and through us. Something put in us uniquely by our Creator. However, the "keeping" of peace is little more than a quick fix that comes at a cost. It's a counterfeit peace.

The peace of God is pure and perfect, much like hope and joy. It goes beyond what we can conjure up on our own. Beyond what we can easily articulate or explain. Those three things, hope, joy, and peace, much like faith, very often just don't make any logical sense.

I love this quote by Francis Chan: "Something is wrong when our lives *make sense* to unbelievers."

It's time to get our hopes up!

It's time to start living fully aware and awake of the goodness of God that is all around us. He is always speaking, He is always moving, and He is always working on our behalf. Do we have eyes to see it? Or are we blind to it because of our unbelief, our lack of faith, or our propensity to grumble and complain? Have we defined or limited God by what we think He *isn't* doing, rather than being open and receptive to what He *is* doing? Are we more *dis*couraged by what we perceive as silence or lack than we are *en*couraged by His very *word* and His faithful provision?

Listen, questioning the goodness of God is a complete waste of time, and it will get you nowhere other than further down the path of misery and despair. And that's a horrible place to be. On the other hand, pressing into the goodness of God and renewing your mind to that one brilliant truth that *God is good* will change your life.

For the believer who desires to *re*-present Jesus to the world in truth and power, hope is not an option. Joy and peace are not options either. They're upgrades, and they're free. But free is not the same as automatic. I have witnessed plenty of Christians who have received salvation but are running low on hope, disconnected from joy, and struggling to find peace. They may be going to heaven, but their "tree of life" is barely producing any fruit. That's not how we were meant to live as believers. Jesus said in John 10:10 (CSB), "I have come that they may have life and have it in abundance." Too many are living without the abundance part of this truth. The abundant life is built with the bricks of surrender and the mortar of obedience.

Another wise insight I recently heard is that if we "experience" any shortage of the abundant life Jesus came to give us, it's always a problem on our end. Never on His. But the loving-kindness of our God is what leads us to repentance. That "ah-ha" moment where we realize, "I've got to think about this differently, and I've got to do this differently."

When we embrace the fact that God's thoughts are higher than our thoughts and His ways are higher than our ways (Isaiah 55:8–9), we are submitting to His lordship. Submitting to His lordship is where we begin to see His goodness more prolifically. His

> *The abundant life is built with the bricks of surrender and the mortar of obedience.*

thoughts and His ways are rich and abundant and available to us! His thoughts and His ways are transformative!

Earnestly seeking and pursuing the presence, which is the person of Jesus and the Holy Spirit of God, is where we discover abundant life. It's where we renew our minds, knowing we have been given the "mind of Christ" (1 Corinthians 2:16). It's where we align our will to His ways, His ways of living, being, doing, seeing, and loving.

Joy-infused hope that results in peace is the reality of the goodness of God being present and prevalent in our lives. And that reality changes everything. Living in the presence and fully awake and aware of the goodness of God is where we will see our hope, our joy, and our peace exponentially increase. Others will see it too. This kind of transformative work of the Holy Spirit in us will draw others in to get a closer look, where they, too, can "taste and see that the Lord is good" (Psalm 34:8, NIV). What a way to live!

We are daughters of the King, who is the "King of kings and the Lord of lords." He reigns supreme over everything. As His daughters, there is nothing that we will ever need that He hasn't already provided. We are His chosen ones, adopted into the family of God and grafted into the house of Israel. His promises are for us. His declarations of love and blessing are for us as well.

One of my favorite passages is in Isaiah chapter 60. It says, "Arise and shine for your light has come and the glory of the Lord rises upon you. See, darkness covers the earth and thick darkness is over the peoples, *but* the Lord rises upon *you* and His glory appears over *you*" (vv. 1–2, NIV, emphasis mine).

For me, one of the most important words in these two verses is the word "but." Is the world fraught with darkness? *Yes*. Are there people fraught with darkness? *Yes. But… !* There is a bright and glorious light! His name is Jesus, and His light is on *us*. Not only in us but *on* us. His glory shines through *us*. Can there be a more marvelous privilege? Can there be a higher honor? Can there be a greater calling?

Jesus said to His disciples, "You are the light of the world" (Matthew 5:14, NIV). *We* are the light of the world! And we are meant to shine *in* the darkness, not hide from the darkness. Don't we know that in every way light is superior to darkness? We are to be that superior shining light in a dark world that changes the environment and shifts the atmosphere. When a light is turned on in a dark room, there is an undeniable change that takes place. What couldn't be seen can now be seen. To be the "light of the world" is to be a change agent. To illuminate the goodness of God in ways the world has never seen before.

Paul wrote to the believers in Colossians 1 that there was a mystery now revealed: "Christ in you, the hope of glory" (v. 27, NIV). We are to be the light of the world because Christ is in us and He is our hope. Our hope for His glorious return, our hope for heaven, and our hope for living in the power of the gospel today.

> *We are to be the light of the world*
> *because Christ is in us,*
> *and He is our hope for living*
> *in the power of the gospel today.*

Listen, I praise God that Jesus is coming again. But He's already been here once. And what His first coming has done for us is no less important than what His second coming will do. We live *in* hope because of His first coming. We live *with* hope because of His second.

It's time to step fully into our royal identity as daughters of the King. We were created to live abundant lives rich with hope, joy, faith, and love. Our inheritance is secure, and our resources are endless. Nothing that God has purposed for us to do or to be is impossible. He provides it all. Everything we need to live a life of victory.

As the old hymn so beautifully articulates, "His love has no limit; His grace has no measure. His power has no boundary known unto men. For out of His infinite riches in Jesus, He giveth and giveth and giveth again."

You are loved. You are seen. You are known. And you are able. It's time to stand up and wear the crown.